Unmaking Merlin

Anarchist Tendencies in English Literature

Unmaking Merlin

Anarchist Tendencies in English Literature

Elliot Murphy

Winchester, UK
Washington, USA

First published by Zero Books, 2014
Zero Books is an imprint of John Hunt Publishing Ltd., Laurel House, Station Approach,
Alresford, Hants, SO24 9JH, UK
office1@jhpbooks.net
www.johnhuntpublishing.com
www.zero-books.net

For distributor details and how to order please visit the 'Ordering' section on our website.

Text copyright: Elliot Murphy 2013

ISBN: 978 1 78279 575 9

A CIP catalogue record for this book is available from the British Library.

Design: Lee Nash

Printed in the USA by Edwards Brothers Malloy

We operate a distinctive and ethical publishing philosophy in all
areas of our business, from our global network of authors to
production and worldwide distribution.

CONTENTS

Acknowledgements

The staff at Liverpool's Central Library deserve my thanks for kindly helping me with numerous book requests. I am also grateful to Nottingham's volunteer-run independent community, the Sumac Centre, for granting me invaluable assistance through its dense anarchist library. My fellow linguist at UCL, Lars Stromdahl, provided useful and insightful discussions about some of the literary figures in the book and went out of his way to proofread earlier versions. Lastly, my thanks and love must go to the true revolutionary of the family, my sister Lydia, for providing me throughout the preparation of this book with excellent company and even better food.

Preface

For all us sons of earth, the enemy is the reigning despot of heaven, whether that despot is the Olympian, as he has been for the last ten thousand years, or this new Triad of Cruelty, Love, and Lies, who will rule for the next two thousand years.

John Cowper Powys[1]

Anarchism is a broad river with various currents, but in popular imagination and a good deal of scholarship it is commonly misunderstood as being synonymous with disorder and rampant violence. Joseph Conrad, for instance, immortalised the anarchist as a violent fanatic seeking the destruction of civilisation in *The Secret Agent*. Raymond Williams points out in his study *Keywords* that the earliest uses of 'anarchism' 'are not too far from the early hostile uses of Democracy.'[2] But as the enigmatic protagonist of Alan Moore's *V for Vendetta* explained, 'Anarchy means "without leaders"; not "without order."'[3] Colloquial meanings of 'anarchy' (disorder, chaos, bedlam) should not be confused with 'anarchism' ('a decentralized and self-regulating society consisting of a federation of voluntary associations,' as Peter Marshall summarised it in his classic study) – indeed, like Proudhon, most anarchists are 'firm friend[s] of order.'[4] The resistance of the oppressed, the authors of Ephesians also understood, 'is not against flesh and blood, but against the rulers, against the authorities, against the world powers of this dark world and against the spiritual forces of evil in the heavenly realms.'[5] In short, anarchism (or libertarian socialism, depending on your philosophical bent) calls for socialism in the political and economic realm (workers' control over production within a non-hierarchical federation of workers' councils) whilst placing strong emphasis on individual freedom, though it goes beyond liberalism in its rejection of state power. Anarchism is also perhaps more emotive than traditional socialism or Marxism, with more importance being placed upon individual creativity (hence why Neo-Impressionists like Seurat and Pissarro were sympathetic to it).[6]

The life-long anarchist and literary critic George Woodcock explained in 1944 that anarchism 'is not a creed of terror and destruction, of social chaos and turmoil, of perpetual war between the individuals within society; it is not nihilism. On the contrary, it is the opposite of all these; a doctrine based on the idea of natural order within society, and of peace between individuals who respect their mutual freedom and integrity. It is the faith of the complete man, growing to fulfillment through social, economic and mental freedom.'[7] Likewise, after the assassination of Tsar Alexander II in 1881, medical student Sophie Bardina was interviewed by *L'Express*, and said of those responsible: 'Yes, we are anarchists, but for us, anarchy does not signify disorder, but harmony in all social relations; for us, anarchy is nothing but the negation of oppressions which stifle the development of free societies.'[8]

Unlike a great number of studies concerning English literary history, the primary intention of this book is to focus on the neglected and repressed indigenous anarchist tradition of the British Isles, attending to those concerns of authors which strike me as exhibiting what John Cowper Powys and Bertrand Russell called anarchist 'tendencies.' Though the book is almost entirely limited in focus to those authors who have, at one point or another, explicitly defined themselves as anarchists, these tendencies are sometimes indirect or unintentional. Anarchist strains of thought, for instance, have been convincingly found in the ninth-century Najdite Muslims of Basra, the mystical late-medieval anarchists the Brethren of the Free Spirit, and one can easily detect them in the writings and actions of the Diggers and Ranters of the seventeenth century, along with Rabelais (who influenced Powys) and Étienne de La Boétie during the Renaissance.[9]

The anarchist ideas of nineteenth-century workers have also been neglected by many critics and historians who prefer to focus on crime, family structure, and diet. The Yiddish-speaking Jews of Clydeside and East London were fervent anarchists, and the Russian anarchist Peter Kropotkin's journal *Freedom* is a popular text to this day. However, thanks to the decline of the self-educated culture of pre-war Britain and the rise of consumerist fantasies, anarchism's light has dimmed considerably in the nation's collective memory. The Labour Party's early successes in the 1920s and publications like Beatrice and Sidney Webb's *New Statesman* (which countered the anarchist Alfred Orage's *New Age*) also increased the public's faith in parliamentary 'reform' and undermined calls for extra-parliamentary non-violent civil disobedience. Left-leaning publications like the *New Statesman* continue to drown out Britain's anarchist publications and journals. In a letter to Kingsley Martin, editor of the *New Statesman*, Lancelot Hogben reminded him of the following in the Christmas of 1937: 'Fundamentally, my dear Kingsley, you and your entourage expect your readers to pick up an elusive reference to the seventh mistress of a 17th century minor French poet, and refuse to reckon with the fact that hundreds of people who don't give a damn for your French poet or his mistress know much more about a kilowatt, a calorie or a bacteriophage than you do.'[10]

There are no fixed anarchist principles which an individual need adhere to on fear of expulsion from any accepted anarchist groups. Anarchists instead promote the tendency in human thought to challenge and question all forms of authority, domination, hierarchy and coercion, and work towards dismantling them if they cannot be justified. Anarchists and libertarian socialists have had many goals historically which substantially resonate today with many social movements not explicitly termed 'anarchist' (like important strands of the Green movement in Britain), chief amongst them being: to strengthen public control and involvement in mass media; to transform top-down bureaucracies into the worker-controlled industries; free association between individuals at all levels of society; the promotion of equality and human rights between individuals and protection of the natural environment; a rejection of consumerism, commodification and private property; a rejection of transcendent or divine authority; promoting collective usage of intellectual property ('And if the descendants of the very inventor who constructed the first machine for lace-making, a century ago, were to present themselves to-day in a lace factory in Bâle or Nottingham, and claim their rights, they would be told: "Hands off! this machine is not yours," and they would be shot down if they attempted to take possession of it'[11]); promoting non-violent action against harmful or dangerous measures to members of society or people of other countries; a suspicion of all forms of authority. Once we spell out these aims clearly, and identify the kinds of authority these criteria require to be dismantled, it is easy to see with Kropotkin 'the absurdity of naming a few men and saying to them, "Make laws regulating all our spheres of activity, although not one of you knows anything about them!"'

As much as the feudalists, Ottomans, Bolsheviks and modern liberal democracies despise the rule of the *demos*, so too do they reject the idea that their own existence is harmful and divisive. Much propaganda has been put out over the last century and a half to associate 'anarchism' with chaos, misrule, arson, turmoil, violence and confusion. The Girondins, during the French Revolution, attacked their radical opponents as 'anarchists,' helping to associate further collectivist movements with the same concocted ideology. Nobody owns the label 'anarchist,' of course, and the most vicious terrorist can call himself an anarchist at the same time as a pacifist simply because they share similar long-term goals (such as the abolition of the state). Those who branded themselves 'anarchists' in the 1870s spoke against the dictatorship of the proletariat prophesied by the orthodox Marxists, and instead promoted self-governing collectives to replace state organization. Many activists have applied the anarchist principles of trade union organisation with modern factory systems and a variety of early participatory economics. This was later called anarcho-syndicalism, and was advocated by anti-authoritarian socialists like Antonie Pannekoek and Rosa Luxemburg during the violent rise of the Bolsheviks from 1917-1921.

The pre-war British, US, Latin American, Australian and European range of anarcho-syndicalism aimed to construct a libertarian society without economic or political oppression, achieved through the means of general strike and direct action. The anarcho-syndicalists have traditionally believed that the commune should be the focus of society's organisation, whereas the similar anarcho-communists put more emphasis on trade unionists. But these distinctions will not concern us much: anarchist tendencies of all shading and emphasis will instead be our focus. And though the ideas of many nineteenth-century anarchists were informed by their European classical liberal predecessors, anarchism was not an exclusively European creation. Steven Hirsch and Lucien van der Walt have argued, for instance, that 'anarchism was not a European doctrine that diffused outward. Rather, the movement emerged simultaneously and transnationally, created by interlinked activists on three continents.'[12] Although anarchism had been introduced in South Africa in the 1880s by Henry Glasse, who had worked in Kropotkin's Free Press in London, Korean anarchism emerged independently in the 1920s during the struggles against Japanese imperialism, with a Korean anarchist group in Tokyo publishing the journal *Black Wave* from 1921. Peter Marshall comments that 'Korean students in Shanghai put out a Kropotkinist manifesto, describing the dissolution of rural-urban divisions after the anarchist revolution: villages would have the amenities of cities, and cities the greenery of farming villages; money would be abolished and society as a whole would become artistic.'[13] The 'Korean Makhno' Kim Jwa-Jin established an anarchist administration in the Manchurian province of Shinmin, lasting from 1921-31 until it was overthrown by the Japanese.

Along with the goal of surveying anarchist authors, the governing argument of this book will be that anarchist literature has been overlooked, even shunned, in Britain's academic and literary circles. One might, with the anarchist poet Herbert Read, ask why:

> I do not see why intellectuals like myself, who are not politicians pledged to an immediate policy, should not openly declare ourselves for the only political doctrine which is consistent with our love of justice and our need for freedom.[14]

But as David Goodway recognises (echoing the political critic and anarchist Noam Chomsky's seminal essay 'The Responsibility of Intellectuals'), the answer is all too clear:

> Anarchism did not offer intellectuals the social and political rewards which the other forms of socialism did. No positions of power or influence were awarded by anarchism either in struggle for or after the attainment of a free society.[15]

And here is a related view from a *Truthdig* essay by Chris Hedges:

> Most professors of literature, who read the same books I read, who study the same authors, are to literature what forensic medicine is to the human body. These academics seem to spend more time sucking the life out of books than absorbing the profound truths the authors struggle to communicate. Perhaps it is because academics, sheltered in their gardens of

privilege, often have hyper-developed intellects and the emotional maturity of twelve-year-olds. Perhaps it is because they fear the awful revelations in front of them, truth that, deeply understood, would demand they fight back. It is easier to eviscerate the form, the style, and the structure with textual analysis and ignore the passionate call for our common humanity.[16]

The Victorian writer and artist William Morris thought likewise. When offered a Professorship of English Literature at Oxford in 1886, he wrote to the newspapers to 'protest emphatically. For the result would be merely vague talk about literature, which would teach nothing. Each succeeding professor would strive to outdo his predecessor in "originality" on subjects whereon nothing remains to be said. Hyper-refinement and paradox would be the order of the day ... Philology can be taught, but "English literature" cannot.'[17]

Finally, Neil Faulkner adds in a collection of essays on the corporatisation of Britain's educational system that the characteristics of the modern university include:

a growing fragmentation of knowledge through increasingly refined subject specialization;

a retreat from holistic, generalising, and contextualising perspectives within individual subject specialisms;

a growing dichotomy between abstract/generalising theory and operational/vocational knowledge;

a rationing of access to abstract/generalising theory especially within the spread of educational provision for the working class;

the marginalisation, or outright exclusion, of radical critiques and perspectives.[18]

The neglect of anarchist and radical literature stems primarily from these factors, and is reflected in everything from the reading list of undergraduates to the debates in prominent literary journals. As well as focusing on this neglect, I also intend to present arguments why anarchist literature should be given special attention in literary and political discussions, and to explore ways in which its revival could influence how notions like politics and authority are viewed in neoliberal Britain.

Maintaining his powerful metaphor, I will also attempt in the following pages to explore Colin Ward's argument that 'an anarchist society ... is always in existence, like a seed beneath the snow, buried under the weight of the state and its bureaucracy.'[19] This liberating viewpoint, developed by numerous English writers, leads to the practical consequence that the task of the anarchist is to dismantle the current system of coercive institutions in order for the historically repressed libertarian society to flourish. Picasso detected parallel forces at work during human maturation, believing that 'Every child is an artist. The problem is how to remain an artist once we grow up.'[20] Or, as another Pablo put it, we must strive 'to make the world worthy of its children.'[21] Complementing Picasso's concern for individual initiative, the anarchist and sculptor Eric Gill, a close friend of Herbert Read's, often repeated the maxim of the Anglo-Tamil art historian Ananda Coomaraswamy, that 'the artist is not a special kind of man, but every man is a special kind of artist.'[22] Simon Nicholson, writing in a journal of design and engineering in 1972, deplored the consequences of believing otherwise:

Creativity is for the gifted few: the rest of us are compelled to live in the environments constructed by the gifted few, listen to the gifted few's music, use the gifted few's inventions and art, and read the poems, fantasies and plays by the gifted few. This is what our education and culture conditions us to believe, and this is a culturally induced and perpetuated lie.[23]

There have recently been a number of successful studies of anarchist history (Alex Butterworth's *The World That Never Was* is probably the most prominent), though few have explored the largely shunned literary side of anarchism. More recent publications such as Dan Jellinek's *People Power* and Owen Jones's *Chavs* consider, respectively, 'unrepresentative democracy' and 'the demonization of the working class' exclusively through the lens of contemporary leftist journalism. My intention is rather to explore these and other issues relevant to a critique of neoliberalism through the lens of literature and political philosophy.

I

Occupy Catalonia

*The invasion of money into everyday life is something the Belgians
left us as a mark of love.*
Sony Lab'ou Tansi[1]

In 1791, the Dutch conservative patrician Gijsbert van
Hogendorp predicted that the countries of the Enlightenment
would head in one of two directions. The first was the way of
church and state, which believed in 'a right government to be
exercised by one or several persons over the mass of people, of
divine origin and supported by the church.' The other was the
way of those who thought that the power of the state was illegitimate 'except that arising from the free consent of all those who
submit to it', and that 'all persons taking part in government
[should be] accountable for their actions.'[2] The first of these
directions led to the eighteenth-century London elite, which was
'one of the most unaccountable, unrepresentative and inhumane
ever known', as Lindsey German and John Rees characterise it.
Its oligarchy's 'main aim was the creation of fabulous wealth,
regardless of the human or social consequences.'[3]

The second of these directions led in the nineteenth century to
anarchism, which is, in Bertrand Russell's words, 'the ultimate
ideal, to which society should continually approximate.'[4]
Though they disagreed on many things, John Dewey complemented Russell's perspective on authority when he made the
following archetypal anarchist claim: 'When external authority is
rejected, it does not follow that all authority should be rejected
but rather that there is need to search for a more effective source
of authority.'[5] Emma Goldman, a more forceful proponent of
anarchism, held that it 'leaves posterity free to develop its own

particular systems, in harmony with its needs.'[6] An inspiration to Goldman, Gustav Landauer expressed his contempt for the level to which ideological and propaganda systems have indoctrinated the public with the idea that the state is legitimate, somehow part of the natural world. He subsequently made a distinction between folk identity and state identity, refusing to equate the German people with the actions of the state.[7] Structures of domination and hierarchy, to the anarchists, are fundamentally illegitimate and should be dismantled. Structures of co-operation and mutual aid should instead be promoted. The Genevan political philosopher Jean-Jacques Rousseau believed that the arbitrary power of government is 'by its nature illegitimate,' being a product, as Kropotkin summarised the Mikhail Bakunin's view, 'of religion, belongs to a lower state of civilization, [which] represents the negation of liberty, and spoils even that which it undertakes to do for the sake of general well-being.'[8]

Complementing van Hogendorp's two paths of political revolution, Kropotkin stated: 'All through the history of our civilization two contrary traditions, two trends have faced one another; the Roman tradition and the national tradition; the imperial and the federal; the authoritarian and the libertarian.'[9] Kropotkin presented the state as a primary example of authoritarianism, and workers' cooperatives, guilds and parishes as examples of libertarianism. The principal founder of modern sociology, Max Weber, also noted that, 'Like the political institutions historically preceding it, the state is a relation of men dominating men, a relation supported by means of legitimate (i.e. considered to be legitimate) violence.'[10] Even the least oppressive state, Bakunin stated, is still 'criminal enough in its dreams.' As they emerge from the documentary and historical record, heads of state, claimed Erasmus in his *Adagia*, resemble not cool her-kings worthy of awe and deep contemplation, but ant 'the terrible reproach that Achilles hurls at Homer, "people-devouring kings".'[11]

Socialism, as Russell argued, is less a set of strict doctrines and more of a tendency in human nature. The libertarian socialist and anarchist is a socialist of a certain kind. In the words of Adolph Fischer, one of the Chicago martyrs, executed in 1887 after the Haymarket riots, 'every anarchist is a socialist, but every socialist is not necessarily an anarchist.'[12] Libertarian socialism goes further than traditional socialism however, since it's goal is to dismantle all forms of hierarchy and oppression. Although, while essentially interchangeable, the terms differ somewhat in that 'anarchism' implies a society with no state, whilst 'libertarian socialism' implies not only a society with no state, but one in which individual liberties and human rights are protected and promoted. The following pages adopt these assumptions as a general framework of interpretation. But they have not been written simply to argue the 'case for anarchism'; this has been done countless times before. I intend rather to explore anarchist philosophy in the light of certain historical and contemporary case studies and works of literature.

As mentioned, a suspicion of authority is a defining feature of anarchist and left-libertarian literature. In his biography of William Blake, E. P. Thompson identifies the Romantic within the tradition of antinomianism (bearing many similarities with Leo Tolstoy's later development of Christian anarchism), which rejected externally-imposed moral authority and instead embraced Immanuel Kant's maxim of adhering only to the laws of 'the starry heavens above and the moral law within.'[13] Himself a libertarian communist, Thompson saw the following verse as Blake's 'most concise expression of antinomian doctrine':

When Satan first the black bow bent
And the Moral Law from the Gospel rent
He forgd the Law into a Sword
And spilld the blood of Mercys Lord.[14]

Similar approaches to authority are developed in perhaps the most celebrated anarchist text of modern times, William Morris's *News from Nowhere*. For Kropotkin, it is 'perhaps the most thorough, and deeply anarchistic conception of future society that has ever been written' – a conclusion generally accepted by most anarchist historians but ignored by subsequent Marxist literary 'theorists' who focus on the text's potential for erotic or historicist readings.[15] The anarchist George Woodcock also saw in *News from Nowhere* 'a thoroughly anarchist world.'[16] In Morris's future England, the anarchist seeds beneath the snow have been vigorously cultivated and Oxford 'has reverted to some of its best traditions ... It is real learning, knowledge for its own sake ... which is followed there, not the Commercial learning of the past.'[17] Unlike the plain-speaking anti-intellectualism of the anarchists (which Morris displayed sympathy with by parodying Alfred Tennyson's elitism in his play *The Tables Turned*), academics had previously 'affected an exaggeration of cynicism in order that they might be thought knowing and wordly-wise.'[18]

But contrary to the usual labelling of Morris's novel, it is not anarchism which is utopian but rather capitalism and 'representative democracy' (neither representative nor democratic). To take a recent example of representative democracy at work in Britain, 'more MPs voted to oppose the government over the proposed ban on fox-hunting than did over the invasion of Iraq – perhaps evidence that to those who supposedly represent the British people, animals are more important than (un)people.'[19] In light of the rhetorically passionate love of democracy and human rights our leaders have, as well as Labour MP Tristram Hunt's confession that the US is a place 'where miracles happen' as a result of Obama's election, it would be hard for the socialist or anarchist to match the dazzling euphoria displayed by the spokesmen of state capitalism.[20]

All governments, writes Edmund Morgan in *Inventing the*

People, require the 'make believe' of freedom and the delusion that 'the people *have* a voice or make believe that the representatives of the people *are* the people.'[21] In 1919, Stanley Baldwin, later coalition PM, donated one-fifth of his personal wealth to the Treasury to help pay off the national debt and create jobs. It is hard to imagine any MP today, let alone a member of the Cabinet and Britain's most recent coalition PM, attempting something similar. As the MPs' expenses scandal revealed, British representatives believed taxpayer's money would be better used to spend £57,000 on Brian Binley's 'rent,' which he was paying to his own company. Sir Menzies Campbell claimed £10,000 to redesign his London flat, and William Hague's mortgage interest payments of £1,200 per month were also payed by the taxpayer. But in 2011, the public was forced to feel the blow of the banking crisis, not the 70 MPs who were implicated in the scandal. The Child Trust fund was abolished, maternity grants were cut, and pension credits were frozen. Later that autumn, the winter fuel allowance was slashed, leading to a situation whereby the health of the elderly was compromised. In January 2012, people under 35 stopped receiving housing benefit unless they shared a house, and Cameron later cut benefits for those under 25. Pension cuts will not have their full effect until 2015. Britain, as Stephen Armstrong puts it in his excellent *The Road to Wigan Pier Revisited*, has become the 'NeoCon poster boy.'[22]

The Conservative's usual mixture of spending cuts is having a drastic effect on living standards, with a recent study by Save the Children revealing how many parents are now having to choose between heating their home and feeding their family. In 2011 the Office for National Statistics compared data from local authorities and revealed the people in Manchester, Liverpool and Blackburn die ten years younger than people in Kensington and Chelsea. The BBC reported in May 2013 that, based on disposable income, Nottingham is the poorest city in Britain, with many surviving on beans on toast to make ends meet.[23]

Speke, in Merseyside, used to be a green land of small farmhouses. In 1933, Liverpool city architect Sir Lancelot Keay planned to create a new town from the land, building houses, public baths, a library, cinema, theatre and concert hall. Speke was designed to be a self-contained community unit, with the new industrial estate providing jobs. By the 1950s its population was 25,000 and it had become 'a model for self-contained municipal housing estates throughout the world.'[24] By the late 1970s, the factories had closed, like Dunlop and Standards, while Ford was cutting its workforce. DWP minister Chris Grayling referred to it as Britain's Baltimore. Life expectancy on the Hunts Cross side of Speke Boulevard is ten years higher than those in Speke, due, as the Office for National Statistics put it, to 'income deprivation, socio-economic status and health behaviour.'[25] In the south, life expectancy typically falls by one year for every stop travelled east on the Jubilee Line from Westminster. All of this provides a good argument in favour of Karel Williams's suggestion. Professor of Accounting and Political Economy at Manchester University's Business School, she believes that manufacturing should be treated the way we currently treat finance, offering incentives and rebates to firms that provide social benefits (investment, employment, etc.).

Since Labour introduced benefit sanctions in April 2000, an estimated 20,000 people per month have had benefits withdrawn, often for months. Sanctions are carried out even if people turn up late for interviews at the Jobcentre. Indeed, the friendly 'Plus' after the title of many Jobcentres doesn't seem to be beneficial to anyone except the public relations industry. The *Guardian* reported in April 2011 that a whistleblower claimed that his Jobcentre staff tried to meet their weekly target of three people per week for sanctioning, as part of a 'culture change' since the coalition came to power, which, with its entrepreneurial urge, has encouraged competition between advisers, teams and regional offices.[26] Long gone are the days of Rowntree's third round of poverty research, which in 1950 concluded that the welfare system had eradicated both absolute and relative poverty in Britain. The attacks on Britain's manufacturing sector have played a major role in the increase of poverty: In 1950, the UK accounted for over 10% of global exports, but by 2009 that figure had fallen to less than 3%.

These are just some of the effects neoliberal economics has had on British cities since the late 1970s. In the US, Chris Hedges has defined the 'sacrifice zones' of corporate capitalism as 'those areas in the country that have been offered up for exploitation in the name of profit, progress, and technological advancement.'[27] For instance, the utopic principles of American exceptionalism have applied as efficiently at home as they have abroad, since 'by 1889 the buffalo population of North America had been reduced to one thousand from more than fifty million in 1830, wiping out the primary food source for the western Indian tribes and reducing them to beggars.'[28] The story of American decline, for Hedges, is one of 'unchecked and unfettered corporate power, which has taken our government hostage, overseen the dismantling of our manufacturing base, bankrupted the nation, and plundered and contaminated our national resources. Once communities break down physically, they break down morally.'[29]

Technological advancement is not necessarily tied to these forms of exploitation and devastation, as many radicals throughout history have pointed out. The Luddites, for instance, condemned only that technology which was 'hurtful to Commonality.' And the poet and author of 'The Mask of Anarchy' Percy Shelley, though a student and advocate of natural science, nevertheless recognised the alienating effects of technological advance: 'We want the creative faculty to imagine that which we know ... The cultivation of those sciences which have enlarged the limits of the empire of man over the external world, has, for of the poetical faculty, proportionally circumscribed those of the internal world.'[30] Although the 'Mask' is often used by activist movements across Britain, Shelley was far from an anarchist. Unlike Thomas Paine, who believed the state in its ideal form should do no more than head 'the management of the affairs of a nation,' Shelley was at all times in favour of the government and supported violence only as a last resort, hoping to inspire 'Spirit, Patience, Gentleness' amongst his readers, as he puts it in the 'Mask.'[31] He explained in a letter that he was interested in appealing 'from the passions to the reason of men.'[32] Shelley therefore approved of the authority of the state, so long as it was used to 'outspeed' the 'Panic' of a violent society. Passivity was for Shelley the correct path towards a secure nation and the taming of political volcanoes. Like Shelley, 'Paine's fears,' writes Audrey Williamson, 'were centred in the possibility of renewed war.'[33] After the ravages of the American War of Independence, Paine sought a rational, non-violent transition to republicanism. According to his wife, Mary, Shelley was also 'a republican, and loved a democracy. His hatred of any despotism ... was intense.'[34]

It was only until the end of the 1960s that trade unions stopped looking forward to what they called a 'leisure age,' which would be brought about by increased automation. But the rise of privatisation and deregulation in the post-Bretton Woods neoliberal order also brought with it the rise of jobs which have virtually no social function, and exist purely to promote the needs of corporate capitalism: advertising, a large part of tele-sales, armaments, excessive bureaucracy, and so forth.

The story of post-war Britain bears many similarities with the portrait Hedges paints of US neoliberalism. In December 2009 the New Economics Foundation, an independent British think-tank, reported that 'hospital cleaners and child minders added more to society's wealth than the far more highly remunerated bankers and advertisers. While a childcare worker created, on average, £9.50 for every pound she was paid, a City banker would manage to *destroy* £7 for every £1 earned.'[35] In response to New Labour's

50% income tax rate for those earning over £100,000, Andrew Lloyd Webber complained that 'The last thing we need is a Somali pirate-style raid on the few wealth creators who still dare to navigate Britain's gale force waters.'[36]

Not sharing Lloyd Webber's emotional sensitivity, the Nobel Prize-winning economist Joseph Stiglitz reported after the collapse of Lehman Brothers that 'many of the worst elements of the US financial system – toxic mortgages and the practices that led to them – were exported to the rest of the world.' This was done in the name of 'innovation,' though as Stiglitz makes clear, 'some of America's best and brightest were devoting their talents to getting around standards and regulations designed to ensure the efficiency of the economy and the safety of the banking system,' with taxpayers being forced to pay the price.[37]

But the public are not allowed to see the astonishingly clear reality, that Cameron's vision of the pseudo-communitarian 'Big Society' is just as deceptive as Randolph Churchill's campaigns in the 1880s for 'Tory Democracy.' Morris's account of late Victorian capitalism consequently retains its principal insights:

> I hold that the condition of competition between man and man is bestial only, and that of association human ... A mask is worn by competitive commerce, with its respectable prim order, its talk of peace and the blessings of intercommunication of countries and the like; and all the while its whole energy, its whole organized precision is employed in one thing, the wrenching of the means of living from others.[38]

Anarchists like Morris have been extremely sceptical of governmental announcements, and the various forms of publically unifying events which surround state celebrations. Similar to Occupy's imperatives, during a regional congress of socialists and anarchists in 1919, a Russian socialist, Liubim, declared that any society needs leaders and 'heads' to direct it. The anarchists replied: 'Always heads and more heads! Let us try and do without them for once ... We don't want any more of those "heads" who lead us like puppets and who call that "work and discipline."'[39] To take a recent example of the forms of state regalia Morris condemned, the charming Bahraini prince Salman bin Hamad al-Khalifa was invited to the 2011 Royal Wedding in Britain, despite his atrocious human rights record and his oppression of Bahrainis since protests in his country began earlier in the year in February. 'Bahrain has created a state of fear, not a state of safety,' the deputy Middle East director of Human Rights Watch announced. In his democratic pursuit of 'stability' to 'modernise' his state, the British government sees the prince as a 'moderate reformer.'[40] 2011 is consequently remembered as the year of the Royal Jubilee, but in reality there were two jubilees; the one at Buckingham Palace, and the 'people's bailout' organised by the Occupy movement, through which online donations paid off 'distressed' debts like student fees. The concept of jubilee goes back to Biblical times, and though the royals are the official heads of the Church of England, the Occupy movement has proven itself to be far more concerned with selflessness than its political representatives. The philosophy of the coalition government departs radically from what Peter Oborne discusses in the *Daily Telegraph*: 'For almost all of the 20th century, Conservatives were guided by the essential Christian insight that their personal needs, ambitions and egos were the things that mattered least of all. Their lives only had meaning and purpose within the great institutions of church and state.'[41]

Morris's 'utopia' in *News from Nowhere* is an inherently literary exploration of practiced anti-authoritarianism ('It is in no sense of the word a literal picture of the future,' cautions one critic), with a purely imaginative – hence 'Nowhere' – investigation of anarchism's workings and potential life-span yielding different insights from a strictly historical or philosophical approach.[42] His Romantic political essays ('usually neglected, seldom discussed') expand on these themes in less figurative terms, while retaining the anti-intellectualism and plain syntax of his fiction.[43] *To the Working Men of England* decried the 'Greedy gamblers on the Stock Exchange' encouraging military intervention in the Balkans during nationalist revolts against the brutal rule of Turkey (Disraeli's friendly ally).[44] Attempting to match the vernacular simplicity of the Icelandic sagas he deeply admired, 'Morris creates a revolutionary literature because he discovers forms which dramatize the tensions of the revolutionary mind,' John Goode argued, with the unconstrained artistic and political freedoms of Morris's anarchistic worlds being more than a swift departure from the tone of many of his contemporaries (even Edward Bellamy's socialist science fiction novel *Looking Backward* approached legal and ethical issues from a predominantly Marxist perspective).[45]

As Aldous Huxley was also aware, literary and other artistic forms of political exploration are the only modes of inquiry which make full use of man's unique imaginative and creative faculties. Nevertheless, Eric Hobsbawm perhaps cheapened anarchism when he commented that it was no coincidence that anarchist Spain was the home of the Romantic tales of Don Quixote, as if other nations, like those in South America or the Caucasus, are at a disadvantage; which, as the last two decades have shown, they plainly aren't. The core attitudes of anarchists do indeed stem from emotion and imagination, but they also crucially stem from an evaluation of society's structure, the division of labour and the nature of hierarchy.

Morris's persistent promotion of artistic ingenuity at first led his literary creations down the path of escapism (with the poems of his 1870 collection *The Earthly Paradise* being viewed by his contemporaries as a retreat from hierarchy and domination into a remote realm of fantasy), though he later stressed the importance of an engaged and active populace in confronting capitalism's 'mastery of and its waste of mechanical power.'[46]

The moving verse of *The Pilgrims of Hope* (1885), for instance, contrasts sharply with his previously measured though detached tranquility:

I see the deeds to be done and the day to come on the earth,
And the riches vanished away and sorrow turned to mirth;
I see the city squalor and the country stupor gone.
And we a part of it all – we twain no longer alone.[47]

It is passages like these that led Harry Pollitt in 1941 to write of Morris's work:

There is not half enough of this type of propaganda to-day. We have all become so hard and practical that we are ashamed of painting the vision splendid – of showing glimpses of the promised land. It is missing from our speeches, our Press and our pamphlets, and if one dares to talk about the 'gleam' one is in danger of being accused of sentimentalism. Yet I am convinced it was this kind of verbal inspiration that gave birth to the indestructible urge which helped the pioneers of the movement to keep fight, fight, fighting for freedom, when it was by no means as easy as it is to-day.[48]

Morris observes with his usual lucidity that whereas 'the socialists hoped to see society transformed into something fundamentally different ... The object of parliamentary institutions, on the contrary, was the preservation of society in its present form.'[49] Though the diction and tone differ, these literary explorations of a libertarian society are strikingly similar in ideology to the pamphlets of the radical Levellers in 1659, who complained:

It will never be a good world while knights and gentlemen make us laws, that are chosen for fear and do but oppress us, and do not know the people's sores. It will never be well with us till we have Parliaments of countrymen like ourselves, that know our wants.[50]

A century earlier, the poet and printer Robert Crowley informed the 1549 parliament of the gentry's hypocrisy in condemning the poor for illicit behavior when they themselves broke the law through their repressive violence:

> They say we must,
> Their judgement trust,
> And obey theyr decrees,
> Although we see,
> Them for to bee
> Against God's verities.[51]

In the same year, participants of Kett's Rebellion in Norfolk reacting to the enclosure of land drew up the Mousehold articles. Though the rebellion contained many schisms between the more oligarchic and wealthier villages and the poorer rebels, all of its members agreed to abolish serfdom and revolutionise English society, 'Taking power from the lords and placing it instead within the village.'[52]

Throughout the history of England's democratic struggles there have been various manifestations of a society based on justice and not profit, on equality and not power, on 'what the Bible calls "love", the trade unionist "solidarity", the social "fraternity",' as Charles Poulson writes in his conclusion to *e English Rebels*.[53] The Levellers represented one particuly religious variant, though it was hardly less intoleran of oppression and power than other, more secular movements. The parliamentarians and clergy, on the other hand, preferred ot to think of the people as 'part of the nation': 'When we mentin the people we do not mean the confused promiscuous body of the people,' wrote Marchamont Nedham, one of their chief spokesmen.[54] The historian Henry Brailsford wrote that 'there had been nothing like this spontaneous outbreak of democracy in any English or continental army before this year of 1647, nor was there anything like it hereafter till the Workers' and Soldiers' Councils met in 1917 in Russia' – who were subsequently crushed by Leninist oppression and imprisonment.[55] There is a distinct parallel between modern socialist, anarchist and Church group activists on the one hand, and the Quakers, Ranters, Levellers, Agitators, Diggers, Clubmen and Seekers of the seventeenth century on the other: they all exist in an effort to change t state and the dominant economic and political power highly comparable grounds. When it comes to the latt ons, what is striking is the commonality of their p objectives (law and education reform, abolition of ith ough they differed substantially the methods they used ve these objectives.

ost radical sectarian groups of the period were the ike the liberation theologians after them, for Propagating the Gospel' were set up in Wales f England, where the Quakers were first estab- t came out of the North,' said the MP for Sou 'are the greatest pests of the nation.'[56] 'But the an rs,' writes Christopher Hill, 'were often nordain s, and the whole atmosphere of the eration was too rad al to be acceptable to the Presbyterian rgy or the gentry.'[57] The objective of spreading the egalitarian ssage of the gospels was, according to Clement Walker, 'to ch anti-monarchical seditious doctrine to the people' and 'to i e rascal multitude and schismatical rabble against all men o quality in the kingdom, to draw them into associations an ations with one another in every country and with the Ar ll lords, gentry, ministers, lawyers, rich and pea inerant craftsmen soon became radical prea freedom. But the idea that the most refined gentleman should rule above the hushed majority lives on into the present. It was sustained by John Locke and John Stuart Mill, who warned of the 'tyranny of the majority,' who should be governed by the 'more pronounced individuality of those who stand on the higher eminences of thought.'[59] The Labour minister Douglas Jay announced in 1937 that 'in the case of nutrition and health, just as in the case of education, the gentleman in Whitehall really does know better what is good for people than the people know themselves.'[60]

The demise of radicals like the Ranters eventually came in the early 1650s, as the subjection of the rank and file to state repression and lack of organisation left them open to failure. In 1656, William Bond, one of the remaining Ranters from Wiltshire, stated there was 'no God or power ruling over the planets, no Christ but the sun that shines upon us; ... if the Scriptures were a-making again then Tom Lampire of Melksham would make as good Scriptures as the Bible.'[61] Between the years of 1641 and 1660, the press was strictly censored. Nevertheless, according to Richard Overton's radical pamphlet of 1649, 'The Humble Petition,' men's liberties are lost when they are 'kept from making noise.' The government should 'hear all voices and judgments' by removing the 'least restraint upon the Press,' as liberty was not to be enjoyed without 'speaking, writing, printing, and publishing their minds freely.'[62]

The revered Dutch philosopher Baruch Spinoza, in his *Theologico-Political Treatise* of 1670, in a chapter called 'That In a Free State Every Man May Think What He Likes, and Say What He Thinks,' discussed how 'every man is by indefeasible natural right the master of his own thought.'[63] But, like Thomas Hobbes and John Milton, Spinoza believed the state has the 'right to treat as enemies all men whose opinions do not, on all subjects, entirely coincide with his own.'[64] The lofty, pious odes of Milton's *Paradise Lost* and *Paradise Regained* poems were not his only contribution to intellectual life. Without doubt 'several passages of the *Areopagitica*, which are ritualistically quoted to the exclusion of all else, carry implications of majestic breadth, but no one who reads him with care should refer to "Milton's dream of free speech for everybody."'[65] For Leonard Levy, Milton's 'well-advertised tolerance did not extend to the thought that he hated.'[66] He disregarded the liberties of non-Protestants, in his case 'Popery, and open superstition, which as it extirpats all religions and civill supremacies, so it self should be extirpat,' denouncing the 'impious' 'evil' which 'no law can possibly permit.'[67] The Very Reverend W. R. Matthews, Dean of St. Paul's, had discussed the exaggerated note of Milton's libertarianism, pointing out that the blind bard 'did not support freedom of religious debate for Catholics, Anglicans, Atheists or non-Christians,' and 'it is clear that Milton himself would have excluded not only the overwhelming majority of Christians but the greater part of the human race from the benefit of his tolerance.'[68] Even the great orator Cicero, regarded as another guardian of democratic virtues, organized killings of labourers who demanded equality, and in his spare time referred to the poor of Rome as 'the dirt and filth,' 'a starving, contemptible rabble,' 'the bilge-water or dregs of the city,' and 'the wicked.'[69]

As with radical pamphlets, dream literature throughout English history has proven to be a viable medium through which authors have engaged in dialogues with classical texts. These texts can often be detected as an influence and a guide, yielding a 'new science' (or understanding, as Geoffrey Chaucer put it) for the audience of medieval poets to interpret their place in the natural world and the hierarchical social structures imposed on them by church and state. In Chaucer's *The House of Fame*, the narrator is guided by an eagle around a glass temple decorated with images of classical heroes. His guide soon begins to expound on the Aristotelian physics behind falling bodies, with Chaucer (unlike Petrarch and the Italian 'humanists') being one of the few medieval poets open to the 'new science' of the

Merton natural philosophers.[70] The work on matter, mechanics, and dynamics by Bradwardine (present in the *Nun's Priest's Tale*), Heytesbury, Strode (to whom Chaucer dedicated *Troilus and Criseyde*) figures in the background as the eagle explores through logical reasoning the physics of sound, pledging 'A preve by experience,' judging matters based on empirical evidence.[71] Chaucer's oeuvre typically frames 'experience' in opposition to 'authority'; a dichotomy which, in *Fame* (with its lack of chapels, monasteries, and paradises) supports a secular appreciation of naturalistic inquiry over the *auctorite* of instinct and purely imaginative literature, and affirms Mikhail Bakunin's belief that an 'instinct for freedom' is a defining feature of human experience. Though Geoffrey restricts the eagle's exposition in order not the distort the poem's artistic merits, it would not be mistaken to describe this as a form of 'popular science,' and one which (like Kropotkin) employs the findings of scientists to undermine the claims of concentrations of domestic power.

By 1614 the English public had a 'bitter and distrustful' attitude towards the gentry, according to John Barclay's *Icon Animorum*.[72] One historian has discovered the response of a Yorkshire village blacksmith to the assassination of the Duke of Buckingham in 1628. Speaking in 1633, he exclaimed: 'The devil go with the King and all the proud pack of them. What care I?'[73] Joseph Beaumont, in his 1648 epic poem *Psyche*, expressed a hope that this popular suspicion of authority would spread:

Time may come ...
When lies alone shall be adorned by
The strange wild faith of its plebeian rout,
Who sooner will believe what soldiers preach
Than what ev'n angels or apostles teach.[74]

This appreciation for 'plebeian' culture and self-organisation can be found throughout the intervening centuries, and in more recent times was expressed most keenly by George Orwell. Joining Morris's denunciation of capitalism (refuting along the way the 'huge tribe of party-hacks and sleek little professors' who equate socialism with 'a planned state-capitalism with the grab-motive left intact'), Orwell praised the workers who collectivized their industry during his visit to Catalonia as civil war spread throughout Spain: 'Waiters and shop-walkers looked you in the face and treated you as equal.'[75] 'The landowners were gone' from La Granja, and the friendliness of the peasants – with their innate 'Anarchist tinge' – 'never ceased to astonish me.'[76] Quite generally, it was understood that 'the Church was a racket pure and simple. And possibly Christian belief was replaced to some extent by Anarchism.'[77] Aragón, too, was 'not far from' 'perfect equality,' since 'snobbishness, money-grubbing, fear of the boss, etc. – had simply ceased to exist,' and 'no one owned anyone else as his master.'[78] Like Morris, Orwell's work exhibited deeply anarchistic sentiments, and the style of both writers, though in many ways polar opposites, exhibited and reinforced core radical concerns through, respectively, an appreciation of the mysteries of nature and a stress on anti-intellectualism.

Spying further important symbolism, Orwell, employing his crisp and sensible prose, noted how the dress code of the anarchists reflected their encouragement of informal relations and rejection of arbitrary privilege, since 'Practically everyone in the army wore corduroy knee-breeches, but there the uniformity ended.'[79] The typical anarchist militia was 'a democracy and not a hierarchy,' attempting to produce 'a sort of temporary working model of a classless society.' Efficient, coherent, and ethical, the militias were 'based on class-loyalty, whereas the discipline of a bourgeois conscript army is based ultimately on fear.'[80]

Victor Serge recounted in *From Lenin to Stalin* Lenin's speech at the opening session of the Second Congress of the Communist International, approving of his brutal clampdown on and imprisonment of dissidents: 'In a few brief strokes, Lenin outlined truly colossal pictures. The word "millions" was on his lips oftener than any other. The abstract human being, the metaphysician, the individual of the anarchist scarcely existed for him.'[81] In an anti-intellectualist display of blunt honesty, Orwell sees through this sort of grandiose authoritarian oratory:

> I have no particular love for the idealized "worker" as he appears in the bourgeois Communist's mind, but when I see an actual flesh-and-blood worker in conflict with his natural enemy, the policeman, I do not have to ask myself which side I am on.[82]

Likewise, Orwell would later speculate in an essay on Charles Dickens that 'Most revolutionaries are potential Tories, because they imagine that everything can be put right by altering the *shape* of society; once that change is effected, as it sometimes is, they see no need for any other.'[83] Kropotkin replies to these concerns: 'We do not deny that there are plenty of egotistic instincts in isolated individuals. We are quite aware of it. But we contend that the very way to revive and nourish these instincts would be to confine such questions ... to any board or committee, in fact, to the tender mercies of officialism in any shape or form. Then indeed all the evil passions spring up, and it becomes a case of who is the most influential person on the board.'[84] Kropotkin consequently denounced the small number of self-labelled anarchists who terrorised Europe during the later decades of the nineteenth century, warning against 'the illusion that one can defeat the coalition of exploiters with a few pounds of explosives.'[85]

This relationship between principle and practice is constantly drawn to the attention of any politically or ideologically motivated movement, and anarchism has been no exception. Though his attack was focused more on anarchist writers like

Hakim Bey and John Zerzan, Murray Bookchin's infamous criticism of what he called 'lifestyle anarchism' in 1995 maintains a certain degree of relevance today (though he seems to suggest there are 'right' and 'wrong' ways to be an anarchist). Any serious anarchist committed to notions of creativity and free speech should welcome alternative lifestyles, modes of dress, new foods and so on, but not at the expense of anti-authoritarian actions. Indeed, they can often work in tandem. We might also argue in favour of what Bookchin calls the polar opposite of 'lifestyle anarchism,' namely 'social anarchism' (what he, perhaps aggressively, sees as 'real' anarchism), so long as it doesn't do away with diminish the essential importance of lifestyle changes. Bookchin writes in *Social Anarchism or Lifestyle Anarchism: An Unbridgeable Chasm?*:

> The 1990s are awash in self-styled anarchists who – their flamboyant radical rhetoric aside – are cultivating a latter-day anarcho-individualism that I will call lifestyle anarchism. Its preoccupations with the ego and its uniqueness and its polymorphous concepts of resistance are steadily eroding the socialistic character of the libertarian tradition ... Ad hoc adventurism, personal bravura, an aversion to theory oddly akin to the anti-rational biases of postmodernism, celebrations of theoretical incoherence (pluralism), a basically apolitical and anti-organizational commitment to imagination, desire, and ecstasy, and an intensely self-oriented enchantment of everyday life ... a state of mind that arrogantly derides structure, organization, and public involvement; and a playground for juvenile antics.[86]

In November 2013 Mark Fisher confessed similar concerns, condemning what he called neo-anarchists, 'whose involvement in politics extends little beyond student protests and occupations, and commenting on Twitter,' and who include many privileged graduate students, typically 'critical theorists' and the like (more on this later):

> 'Left-wing' Twitter can often be a miserable, dispiriting zone. Earlier this year, there were some high-profile twitterstorms, in which particular left-identifying figures were 'called out' and condemned. What these figures had said was sometimes objectionable; but nevertheless, the way in which they were personally vilified and hounded left a horrible residue: the stench of bad conscience and witch-hunting moralism. ... The open savagery of these exchanges was accompanied by something more pervasive, and for that reason perhaps more debilitating: an atmosphere of snarky resentment. The most frequent object of this resentment is Owen Jones, and the attacks on Jones – the person most responsible for raising class consciousness in the UK in the last few years – were one of the reasons I was so dejected. If this is what happens to a left-winger who is actually succeeding in taking the struggle to the centre ground of British life, why would anyone want to follow him into the mainstream? Is the only way to avoid this drip-feed of abuse to remain in a position of impotent marginality?[87]

Like the factory workers of Victorian Lancashire and Glasgow, the Spanish anarchist organisations were characterized more by political action and participation, and not simply this kind of virulent and introverted debate. The CNT and FAI stood for 'Direct control over industry by the workers engaged in each industry,' along with 'Government by local committees and resistance to all forms of centralized authoritarianism.'[88] Not meeting the crude definitions of 'democracy' espoused by Winston Churchill or the communists, these thriving anarchist societies were later destroyed by force for the usual reason: 'If the capitalist republic prevailed, foreign investors would be safe.'[89]

During the Spanish Civil War, British arms were supplied to Franco through the Strait of Gibraltar to help defend British interests in the region against the workers councils and anarchists. Churchill approved of the brutalisation of Spanish workers, and while he was shipping arms to his fascist comrade the British public were sending great numbers of food ships to the Spanish people. The supplies were sent from places such as Liverpool, Tyneside, and Glasgow through groups like Aid Spain, the Quakers, the Salvation Army and Save the Children Fund, and medical supplies soon followed. Churchill, man of the people, despised such measures. Illustrating further the integrity of the Great Powers, the late historian Chris Harman writes that 'the rulers of Western "democracies" were content for Hitler and Mussolini to flout a "non-interventionist" pact, since Franco was no danger to their empires.'[90] In fact, along with Franco, the Prime Minister also defended Stalin during Cabinet meetings. On 14 August 1938, Churchill said in an interview that 'Franco has all the right on his side because he loves his country. Also Franco is defending Europe against the Communist danger – if you wish to put is in those terms. But I, I am English, and I prefer the triumph of the wrong cause. I prefer that the other side wins, because Franco could be an upset or a threat of British interests, and the others no.'[91] The proud Englishman had also told his Cabinet friends in 1914 (reported years later in the press, with any offending phrases omitted):

We are not a young people with an innocent record and a scanty inheritance. We have engrossed to ourselves an altogether disproportionate share of the wealth and traffic of the world. We have got all we want in territory, and our claim to be left in the unmolested enjoyment of vast and splendid possessions, mainly acquired by violence, largely maintained by force, often seems less reasonable to others than to us.[92]

As Churchill understood, the allies went to war in September 1939 'to challenge Nazi Germany's intention to dominate the European continent rather than to create a new democratic order in Europe and, accordingly, as long as Spain maintained its neutrality Franco's regime had nothing to fear.'[93] After Russia urged for Franco's removal and US and British experts proposed to cut back the Allied supplies of Spain's oil to temper its dictators tyranny, Churchill immediately objected: What you are proposing to do is little less than stirring up a revolution in Spain. You begin with oil, you will quickly end in blood ... If we lay hands on Spain ... the Communists become masters of Spain [and] we must expect the infection to spread very fast through both Italy and France.[94]

The Spanish libertarian and anarchist movements during the civil war were based on the assumption of collective ownership of land, with work, enterprise and innovation encouraged through means of free association between individuals. The people's war consequently developed in Barcelona 'not only to defeat the Nationalists but in opposition to the elected Republican government Franco wished to overthrow.'[95] This form of anarcho-syndicalism (which Lenin, not without irony, had earlier denounced as 'merely the twin brother of opportunism') was, to Marshall S. Shatz, 'the most concerted effort the anarchists made to adapt their principles to the structure of modern industry. It sought to achieve the libertarian society by means of trade-union organizations, through which the producers themselves would take over the direction of the economy and replace the coercive machinery of capitalism and the state.'[96] In Barcelona eighty per cent of enterprises were collectivized, and it was decreed that 'The victory of the people will mean the death of capitalism.'[97] Here is Guérin's lengthy assessment of the anarchist structure of the collectives:

The agricultural collectives set themselves up with a twofold management, economic and geographical. The two functions were distinct, but in most cases it was the trade unions which assumed them or controlled them. A general assembly of working peasants in each village elected a management committee which was to be responsible for economic administration. Apart from the secretary, all the members continued their manual labor. Work was obligatory for all healthy men between eighteen and sixty. ... With regard to local administration, the commune frequently called the inhabitants together in general assembly to receive reports of activities undertaken. Everything was put into the common pool with the exception of clothing, furniture, personal savings, small domestic animals, garden plots, and poultry kept for family use. Artisans, hairdressers, shoemakers, etc., were grouped in collectives; the sheep belonging to the community were divided into flocks of several hundreds, put in the charge of shepherds, and methodically distributed in the mountain pastures. ... Rent, electricity, medical care, pharmaceuticals, old-age assistance, etc., were all free. Education was also free and often given in schools set up in former convents; it was compulsory for all children under fourteen, who were forbidden to perform manual labor. ... In some places socialized areas were reconstituted into larger units by voluntary exchange of plots with individual peasants. In most villages individualists, whether peasants or traders, decreased in number as time went on. They felt isolated and preferred to join the collectives. It appears that the units which applied the collectivist principle of day wages were more solid than the comparatively few which tried to establish complete communism too quickly, taking no account of the egoism still deeply rooted in human nature, especially among the women. In some villages where currency had been suppressed and the population helped itself from the common pool, producing and consuming within the narrow limits of the collectives, the disadvantages of this paralyzing self-sufficiency made themselves felt, and individualism soon returned to the fore, causing the breakup of the community by the withdrawal of many former small farmers who had joined but did not have a really communist way of thinking.[98]

There were also successful movements towards self-management inside industry which were just as successful as the agricultural movements, with most factories being organised in a highly efficient manner. The factories also contributed to the fight against fascism, with workers and technicians in Barcelona sending war material to the front.

A study of the collectivisation efforts in Spain during the Civil War was published by the CNT (Confederación Nacional del Trabajo, the anarcho-syndicalist labour unions) in 1937. Amidst the brutal oppression of the Republicans, the study describes the village of Membrilla in the province of Siudad Real: 'In its miserable huts live the poor inhabitants of a poor province; eight thousand people, but the streets are not paved, the town has no newspaper, no cinema, neither a cafe nor a library. On the other hand, it has many churches that have been burned ... Food, clothing, and tools were distributed equitably to the whole population. Money was abolished, work collectivized, all goods passed to the community, consumption was socialized. It was, however, not a socialization of wealth but of poverty.'[99] Membrilla also accommodated refugees and established a small library and craft school. As Orwell would attest in *Homage to Catalonia*, the collectivist efforts of the Spanish anarchists seem to depict humanity as distinct from Marx's quasi-existentialist conception 'of Man in general, who belongs to no class, has no reality, who exists only in the misty realm of philosophical fantasy.'[100] After staying with his wife Eileen at the Hotel Continental in Barcelona, Orwell learnt a great deal about the various anarchist factions and militias in revolutionary Spain: 'I have the most evil memories of Spain, but I have very few bad memories of Spaniards. I only twice remember even being seriously angry with a Spaniard, and on each occasion, when I look back, I believe I was in the wrong myself.'[101]

The German anarchist Augustin Souchy, in his autobiography, describes how during 'the course of collectivization of the village of Membrilla, the sum of 30,000 Pesetas in the tills of the municipality was distributed in equal amounts among the inhabitants before the impecunious communal economy was started. Although the initiative came from the anarcho-syndicalists, there were many instances where members of the socialist union UGT (Union General de Trabajadores – General Workers' Union) participated in communal work.'[102] The CNT report concludes: 'The whole population lived as in a large family; functionaries, delegates, the secretary of the syndicates, the members of the municipal council, all elected, acted as heads of a family. But they were controlled, because special privilege or corruption would not be tolerated. Membrilla is perhaps the poorest village of Spain, but it is the most just.'[103]

An active participant in the Spanish libertarian socialist revolution, the French historian Gaston Leval recorded how, despite a vicious civil war, over sixty per cent of Spanish land was collectively cultivated by peasants without resort to bosses and managers, and without the competitive spirit of capitalism to spur them on. Over eight million people directly or indirectly participated: 'In almost all the industries, factories, mills, workshops, transportation services, public services, and utilities, the rank and file workers, their revolutionary committees, and their syndicates reorganized and administered production, distribution, and public services without capitalists, high salaried managers, or the authority of the state.'[104]

During his literary career in the 1930s, Orwell developed into a critic of political and economic tyranny. Engaging in a form of citizen journalism, he defended the ideals of socialism and what

Howard Zinn referred to as 'the countless small actions of unknown people.' As *The Road to Wigan Pier* clearly demonstrates, Orwell defended 'mutual trust' and fraternity in opposition to the 'abstract' version of 'proletarian solidarity' espoused by the Marxist intellectuals.[105] The first part of *Wigan Pier* has been routinely deemed sentimental by some critics, as Richard Hoggart has pointed out.[106] But Orwell's dexterity in his combination of statistics and description, of text and context, hint at a more salient purpose behind his obsession with the minutiae of ordinary experience and emotion. Indeed, even the strongest critics have applauded the honesty and clarity with which Orwell graphically depicts the plight of the impoverished northerner.

To begin with, the very title of the book can be read as a protest against the uncertain lives of blue-collar workers, since Orwell excitedly anticipates his visit to Wigan Pier in the text, only to discover its ruin upon arrival. On the first page we learn how Orwell is awoken at the Brooker's lodgings by 'the clumping of the mill-girls' clogs down the cobbled street.' Once the sun has risen, many unemployed men fill their days with newspapers and popular literature, with the Scotch miner in particular concerning himself with 'such things as the Yellow Peril, trunk murders, astrology, and the conflict between religion and science.'[107] The Etonians, on the other hand, are often ridiculed by Orwell, who seems to view his own classical education as essentially worthless next to the labourers he investigates. Most cases of dishonesty in Lancashire breed upon the internal politics of everyday social interaction, as opposed to the large-scale propagandistic deceit of the heads of state Orwell condemns in Part II of *Wigan Pier*.

On the nature of private property, the 'inevitable result of the bad system,' Orwell laments, is that 'the lodger has to live in somebody else's house without being one of the family,' stirring in the Brookers a 'jealous attitude' towards the lodgers: Echoing many before him, Orwell concludes that capitalism distorts ordinary family values, with the Brookers slowly acquiring 'a determination not to let the lodger make himself too much at home.'[108] The typical lodger, in the eyes of the Brookers, was someone severely lacking the qualities of the 'good-class "commercial gentleman",' namely paying 'thirty shillings a week and never [coming] indoors except to sleep.'[109] In the mines, too, we read of how a 'sheeplike' mentality dominates the minds of the workers, whose ordinary powers of self-direction are suppressed. In the estates of Liverpool and Sheffield, Orwell is received with 'extraordinary courtesy and good nature,' and 'everyone was astonishingly patient.' Commenting on his 'upper middle class' background, Orwell confesses that '[i]f any unauthorised person walked into *my* house and began asking me whether the roof leaked and whether I was much troubled by bugs and what I thought of my landlord, I should probably tell him to go to hell.'[110]

Moreover, in Orwell's 'early boyhood ... "common" people seemed almost sub-human,' surrounded as he was by people who thought 'the lower classes smell.'[111] In accordance with Lorraine Saunders' contention that 'Orwell's entire political thinking is rooted in a determined belief that the "ordinary" man is nobler than the "cultivated" man,' Jenni Calder observes in her perceptive study of Orwell that he 'found a more decent, vital and attractive kind of humanity amongst working-class people than he ever did amongst the class to which he belonged.'[112] A strong notion of independent agency is built around Orwell's depiction of the working class (as opposed to the form of 'blind' indoctrination the middle classes are typically exposed to). Unlike the natural-born goodwill of the mill-girls and miners, the middle-class snobbishness Orwell was exposed to 'sticks by you til your grave' 'unless you persistently root it out like the blindweed it is.'[113]

Orwell soon after decides to leave the Brookers residence, a decision resulting from a 'feeling of stagnant meaningless decay' instilled by living in 'some subterranean place where people go creeping round and round, just like black beetles, in an endless muddle of slovened jobs and mean grievances.'[114] Taking the train out of town, Orwell spies a young woman 'kneeling on the stones' behind one of the many 'little grey slum houses,' 'poking a stick up the leaden waste-pipe which ran from the sink inside and which I suppose was blocked.' Though many critics have been unconvinced by Orwell's mind-reading abilities in this passage, the stark depiction of such a dull everyday activity by a middle-class outsider is perhaps original in its level of sympathy. Like the tenants of the Brookers, again we are met with a destitute labourer whose arms were 'reddened by the cold,' with Orwell noticing in particular her 'round pale face, the usual exhausted face of the slum girl who is twenty-five and looks forty, thanks to miscarriages and drudgery.' Even newborn life itself, the symbol of marital and financial strength for the middle classes, swings on a vulnerable and delicate pendulum for the workers of Lancashire. Instead of the optimism and aspirations of the stereotypical 'city girl' of the Roaring Twenties, this 'slum girl' had 'the most desolate, hopeless expression I have ever seen.' Consequently, it suddenly 'struck' Orwell 'that people bred in the slums can imagine nothing but the slums,' even if they 'knew well enough what was happening to [them].'[115]

The rugged lifestyle of the typical miner has also made him suspicious of and resilient to what Russell called 'intellectual rubbish'; namely 'the philosophic side of Marxism, the pea-and-thimble trick with those mysterious entities, thesis, antithesis, and synthesis ... I have never met a working man who had the faintest interest in it.'[116] The ordinary man, we are told, has no interest in academic games, but is concerned with issues of decent survival and the condition of his family – and is a nobler person for it, since the 'mysterious' language of the Marxist intellectual only serves to estrange radical ideas from the majority of the population, as more recent writers like Owen Jones and Chris Hedges often point out. It is only the clear tone of Orwell's 'Socialist' which can help the working classes teach themselves of their own power and potential against the 'thousand influences' which deem their subordination necessary.

When the mines are busy on a typical working day, 'the place is like hell, or at any rate like my own mental picture of hell,' with scenes of 'heat, noise, confusion, darkness, foul air' occurring in an 'unbearably cramped place.'[117] The repeated image of windows jammed shut creates a sense of forced enclosure and squalor about the Lancashire tenants. The 'fillers' in the mines have particularly a 'dreadful job,' 'an almost superhuman job by the standards of an ordinary person,' taking on a workload three times the usual rate.[118] Even 'hell' itself can never fully constrain such a level of extraordinary physical aptitude. Demonstrating himself to be an astute pupil of Dickens, Orwell writes how possessing a unique and important skill can elevate one's social and moral standing above the accepted and organised character-istics of the workplace. Indeed, those labourers who find genuine fulfillment in their tasks begin to adopt the aesthetic style of their surroundings, since they 'really do look like iron – hammered iron statues – under the smooth coat of coal dust which clings to them from head to foot.'[119] But it is largely the unique nature of their work which sets the miners apart, since when their faces are clean 'there is not much to distinguish them from the rest of the population.'[120]

The physical prowess needed to mine is, to Orwell, extraor-dinary. The 'bending,' 'travelling,' 'shifting,' 'loading' and 'shovelling' stirs in the author a recognition that '[t]he miner's job would be as much beyond my power as it would be to perform on the flying trapeze or to win the Grand National' ('the work would kill me in a few weeks').[121] This form of ordinary labour is furthermore necessary for extraordinary feats of ingenuity. 'Practically everything we do,' Orwell notices, 'from eating an ice cream to crossing the Atlantic, and from baking a load to writing a novel, involved the use of coal. For all the arts of peace coal is needed; if war breaks out it is needed all the more.'[122] Coal (and hence the labour behind its rise to the surface) is the grist in the artist's mill, the gas which aids the mind of the novelist as they write at night: Orwell has 'got to have' coal for his fire during his writing hours, which 'arrives mysteriously from nowhere in particular, like manna except that you have to pay for it.'[123] One can be ignorant of the miners' existence during these moments of creative solitude or when driving along a country road, but 'in a sense it is the miners who are driving your car forward.' If one were to descend the depths of the mines, watching an ordinary miner at work 'is even humiliating,' since it 'raises in you a momentary doubt about your own status as an "intellectual" and a superior person generally.' Hinting at his own belief in the latent power of the proletariat, it is suddenly 'bought home' to Orwell that 'it is only because miners sweat their guts out that superior persons can remain superior.'[124] Stressing his point, Orwell estimates that in his lifetime he will write thirty novels, 'or enough to fill two medium-sized library shelves.' The average miner, on the other hand, will have produced enough coal 'to pave Trafalgar Square nearly two feet deep or to supply seven large families with fuel for over a hundred years.'[125] As he would soon emphasise in *Homage to Catalonia*, Orwell believed honour is to be found not in fame or authority, but in a level of public service through which work becomes not a chore but rather, as Marx wished, 'life's prime want.'[126]

What is of particular interest to Orwell is that the occurrence of unpaid working hours is common for the average miner, whose 'working shift of seven and a half hours does not sound very long, but one has got to add on it at least an hour a day for "travelling."'[127] By this point in the narrative, the evidence has begun to mount that the stringent and unremorseful capitalist system of fixed working hours is incompatible with the ordinary types of jobs available to the working classes: Hence the 'iniquitous swindle of making the miner pay for the hire of his lamp,' in addition to the 'half a crown a week' he is forced to spend on commuting fares.[128] These nameless 'thousand forces' compel the miner 'into a *passive* role,' converting him into a 'slave of mysterious authority' with 'a firm conviction that "they" will never allow him to do this, that and the other.'[129] Whoever these (state-corporate) forces are, the miner recognises them to be anathema to his own true nature; and, though ordinary life may be squalid ('Quite often you have eight or even ten people living in a three-roomed house'), its typically compassionate nature is revealed to be the feature which strikes Orwell as likely to last far longer than the stench of penury which intrudes upon an otherwise natural arrangement.[130]

2

This Side of Paradise

My faith in the people governing us is, on the whole, infinitesimal;
my faith in The People governed is, on the whole, illimitable.
Charles Dickens[1]

Beyond doubt another complex figure (who can perhaps most
aptly be characterised as an aristocratic anarchist), the early
Aldous Huxley aligned himself closely with Oscar Wilde's
anarchism and aestheticism, and was one of only three out of a
hundred and forty-nine British writers who defended the
Spanish anarchists in the *Left Review*'s 1937 publication 'Authors
Take Sides on the Spanish Civil War.'[2] He was, however, later
influenced by H. L. Mencken's elitist critique of mass democracy
and shifted to an aristocratic authoritarianism. At one point he
even praised eugenics and advocated sterilizing 'the feeble-
minded' and 'half-wits.'[3] He later converted to anarchist
pacifism after hearing of Mussolini's savagery in Abyssinia, and
argued in *Ends and Means* for an anti-consumerist 'non-attached'
personality to be roused before the call of 'Decentralization and
Self-Government' (the title of the book's most esteemed chapter,
in which he explains why 'the state is obviously worthy of
abolition') can be taken seriously.[4] William Propter correspondingly argues in Huxley's 1939 novel *After Many a Summer* that
democracy has to be established independently from the
external influence of a state or big business if arbitrary hierarchies are to be avoided.[5] Placing his anarchist philosophy in a
literary setting not only allowed Huxley to develop his pacifist
and anti-authoritarian ideals, it also helped convert the intellectual formalisms of his essays into highly imaginative and
richly detailed worlds, allowing him to envision and explore the

more ethical and practical consequences of establishing an anarchist society.

The radical tendencies in Huxley's *Island* ('a kind of pragmatic dream,' for him), along with his hatred of war, are also 'undoubtedly anarchist in spirit.'[6] His largely forgotten 'utopian' text concerned, as he told Emma Goldman, 'a satisfactory technique for giving practical realization to the ideal of philosophic anarchism.'[7] On the island of Pala, political revolution goes hand in hand with the patriarch-smashing acts of sexual liberation. Maithuna, 'the yoga of love,' helps the Palanese pay close attention to 'the mystery of the other person – the perfect stranger, who's the other half of your own self.'[8] The literariness of *Island*'s anarchist philosophy yields a certain distance and ambiguity, provoking its readers into extracting and developing Huxley's ideas in more imaginative, thoughtful ways than the sparse prose of *Ends and Means*. Pala, we later find, is 'a federation of self-governing units' with 'no place for any kind of dictator at the head of a centralized government.'[9] There are 'No Alcatrazes here ... No hells on earth and no Christian pie in the sky, no Communist pie in the twenty-second century.'[10] Attempting to create the sort of participatory democracy Michael Albert would approve of, Dr Robert explains to the novel's protagonist, Will, that in the West people spend 'nine-tenths' of their time on

"planes and cars, just foam rubber and an eternity of sitting ... slowly destroy[ing] them."
"So you take to digging and delving as a form of therapy?"
"As prevention – to make therapy unnecessary. In Pala even a professor, even a government [worker's council] official generally puts in two hours of digging and delving each day."
"As part of his duties?"
"And as part of his pleasure."[11]

A similar concern for leisure had earlier encouraged William Morris to observe that, 'If a professional man ... does a little more than his due daily grind – dear me, the fuss his friends make of him! how they are always urging him not to overdo it, and to consider his precious health, and the necessity of rest and so forth! [sic].'[12] Another core principle of anarchism emerges here, which was articulated best by the German linguist and anti-statist Wilhelm von Humboldt. By appealing to the uniqueness of man's creative faculties, he argued that if an artisan produces something beautiful, but does it under external command, 'we may admire what he does, but we despise what he is.'[13] Joshua Hagler also writes in the afterword to his remarkable comic series *The Boy Who Made Silence*, reviving the concerns of Morris: 'I still believe that what one does for money is a compromise with that secret center that compels one's original art-making instinct.'[14] The classical liberal John Ruskin (for whom exploitation was 'the English practice') discussed similar issues in his treatise on Venetian art and architecture, *The Stones of Venice*:

You must either make a tool of the creature, or a man of him. You cannot make both. Men were not intended to work with the accuracy of tools, to be precise and perfect in all their actions. If you will have that precision out of them, and make their fingers measure degrees like cog-wheels, and their arms strike curves like compasses, you must unhumanize them ... On the other hand, if you will make a man of the working creature, you cannot make a tool. Let him but begin to imagine, to think, to try to do something worth doing; and the engine-turned precision is lost at once. Out come all his roughness, all his dullness, all his incapability ... but out comes the whole majesty of him also.[15]

Following in Humboldt's footsteps and abolishing wage slavery, labour on Pala has become fulfilling both helpful to the community and fulfilling to the individual. In the rigid 'education' systems of the West, 'You don't allow your teenagers to work; so they have to blow off steam in delinquency.'[16] It seems to me that it is all the more interesting that these anarchist views are found in a sporadically authoritarian aristocrat like Huxley, and if such a usually bigoted and sexist figure can craft a thoughtful and useful attack on the state, then surely we can expect much more from those who identify themselves as part of the left.

Huxley also often deplored Britain's education system and its 'teach to test' philosophy (a theme to be returned to later):

> Literary or scientific, liberal or specialist, all our education is predominantly verbal and therefore fails to accomplish what it is supposed to do. Instead of transforming children into fully developed adults, it turns out students of the natural sciences who are completely unaware of Nature as the primary fact of experience, it inflicts upon the world students of the humanities who know nothing of humanity, their own or anyone else's.[17]

A liberating education and the kindling of scientific curiosity have been principal drives for many anarchists in their attacks on state power. Kropotkin's brother, Alexander, had written to him years before he came to prominence about the influence of Charles Darwin's *The Descent of Man*. 'Those nice children,' he wrote of the tsarist government, 'simply don't comprehend that it is more dangerous than a hundred A. Kropotkins.'[18] The dissident and democratising effects of science have not gone unnoticed in the past: The Copernican world view subverted the authority of the Church just as much as Jesus's teaching undermined the aggression of the Roman Empire. Still, in large part thanks to the ranking of 'toughness' of disciplines, science can often provide a dangerously neutral moral ground for some.

While many scientists simply prefer exploring formal and mathematical systems to what David Foster Wallace called 'the referential murkiness and inelegance of verbal systems,' the Brazilian philosopher of education Paulo Freire was undoubtedly justified in writing how both students and teachers 'might try to hide in what [they] regard as the neutrality of scientific pursuits, indifferent to how [their] findings are used, even uninterested in considering for whom or for what interests [they] are working.' They 'might treat [the] society under study as though [they] are not participants in it. In [their] celebrated impartiality, [they might] approach this world as if [they] were wearing "gloves and masks" in order not to contaminate or be contaminated by it.'[19]

Nevertheless, Kropotkin was more than justified in stressing the anti-dogmatic nature of anarchism, while Darwin (despite his physical revulsion to Shakespeare in his later years), writing to his friend Henslow, also explained: 'I believe there exists, & I feel within me, an instinct for truth, or knowledge or discovery, of something of the same nature as the instinct of virtue, & that our having such an instinct is reason enough for scientific researches without any practical results *ever* ensuing from them.'[20] This stress on human freedom as distinct from the dictates of ecclesiastical or state power had earlier emerged during the Renaissance, when Pico della Mirandola famously wrote, assuming the role of God speaking to man:

The nature of other creatures is defined and restricted ... you, by contrast ... may, by your own free will ... trace for yourself the lineaments of your own nature ... We have made you a creature neither of heaven nor of earth ... in order that you may, as the free and proud shaper of your own being, fashion yourself in the form you may prefer.[21]

Alongside Huxley's work, another notable anarchist work in the science fiction idiom is Ursula Le Guin's *The Dispossessed*, first published in 1974. It is regrettable that critics have continually downplayed the novel's anarchist underpinnings, preferring to investigate its feminist or ecological themes. Important as these interpretations are, 'the radical political ramifications of the novel remain woefully under explored.'[22] As Dan Sabia puts it, the number of anarchist readings of the novel is 'slim' – a peculiar fact considering the author's own anarchist leanings.[23]

The narrative itself is laden with inventive imagery which often lends the novel a sense of radical moral conviction, with walls, for instance, symbolising above all else the arbitrary national boundaries imposed forcefully by states (and the corruption of human psychology which often results): 'Where [the wall] crossed the roadway, instead of having a gate it degenerated into mere geometry, a line, an idea of boundary. But the idea was real.'[24] The protagonist Shevek, a physicist, is met with 'this curious matter of superiority and inferiority' when exposed to the hierarchical society of the planet Urras (a model of Earth for Le Guin) during his flight there to meet with fellow physicists.[25] In vivid contrast to the libertarian Anarres, the education system on Urras indoctrinates students into becoming passive consumers of conventional pieties. Shevek 'could not imagine a greater deterrent to the natural wish to learn than this pattern of cramming information and disgorging it at demand.'[26] Shevek also rejects the rigorous 'teach to test' philosophy which dominates contemporary education (as Chomsky recently commented on the matter: 'What's the point of being better than someone else?').[27] He instead favours establishing, as John Dewey would put it, 'a rich and challenging environment for the individual to explore, in his own way.'[28] In this connection, we are told that 'Because he refused to compete in games of domination he was indomitable.' Though he admires his students on an intellectual level, 'he felt no great warmth towards any of them. They were planning careers as academic or industrial scientists, and what they learned from him was to them a means to that end.'[29] The children of Anarres, on the other hand, having not been exposed to the wonders of wage slavery or 'education,' are natural anarchists. When Shevek observes the unwillingness of a seven-year old to obey the arbitrary dictates of his older brother, he thinks, with Picasso, that 'The Principle of Superiority did not seem to be well established in his mind yet.'[30] For the mature adults of Urras, the anarchism Shevek lectures on is simply a spectacle, a form of entertainment, not to be used to rid the planet of its great inequalities:

> It seemed that he talked to the same people every time: well dressed, well fed, well mannered, smiling. Were they the only kind of people on Urras? 'It is pain that brings men together,' Shevek said standing up before them, and they nodded and said, 'How true!'[31]

Bertrand Russell, who often expressed a significant degree of sympathy towards anarchism, sided with Shevek insofar as he believed that the purpose of education was to

> give a sense of the value of things other than domination, to help create wise citizens of a free community, to encourage a combination of citizenship with liberty, individual creativeness, which means that we regard a child as a gardener regards a young tree, as something within intrinsic nature which will develop into an admirable form given proper soil and air and light.[32]

Echoing William Blake, Alexander Malinkov preached something similar in New York in the 1870s, namely that 'in every man there is a divine element. It is sufficient to appeal to it, to find the God in man, for no coercion to be necessary. God will settle everything in people's souls and everyone will become just and kind.'[33] The anarchist prince Peter Kropotkin wrote in his memoirs a passage that eloquently draws on this assumption:

> The masses want to know: they are willing to learn; they *can* learn. There, on the crest of that immense moraine which runs between the lakes, as if giants had heaped it up in a hurry to connect the two shores, there stands a Finnish peasant plunged in contemplation of the beautiful lakes, studded with islands, which lie before him. Not one of these peasants, poor and downtrodden though they may be, will pass this spot without stopping to admire the scene. Or there, on the shore of a lake, stands another peasant, and sings something so beautiful that the best musician would envy him his melody, for its feeling and its meditative power. Both deeply feel, both meditate, both think; they are ready to widen their knowledge, – only give it to them, only give them the means of getting leisure.[34]

Just as the state bureaucracy and military are historical residues to anarchists like Colin Ward and Chomsky, the capitalist and religious minds of Urras are to Shevek 'a jumble of intellectual artifacts. On the 'well-meaning' doctor facilitating Shevek's safe transition to Urras, the physicist thinks: 'There were walls all around his thoughts, and he seemed utterly unaware of them, though he was perpetually hiding behind them.'[35] Equally alien to Shevek is the notion of private property: 'His escorts took him into a building and to a room which, they explained, was "his."'[36] This world where the population is assigned the role of misinformed spectators deeply troubles Le Guin's protagonist. The excessive furniture and luxurious bathtub and fireplace in Shevek's room remind him 'of a kind of ultimate apotheosis of the common People are indoctrinated into 'performing leisure', as Thorstein Veblen put it in his less figurative *The Leisure Class*, and Shevek soon grows tired of the radio on Urras after he susses that 'its basic function was advertising things for sale,' since the elites of Urras 'think if people can possess enough things they will be content to live in prison. But I will not believe that. I want the walls down. I want solidarity.'[38] So does Chris Hedges, who writes in a *Truthdig* essay that the majority of consumer goods are 'squalid little monuments to our selves. The more we strive to amass power and possessions, the more intolerant and anxious we become.'[39]

In his classic *The Art of Loving*, Erich Fromm explained presciently that modern happiness 'consists in "having fun."' Having fun lies in the satisfaction of consuming and "taking in" commodities, sights, food, drinks, cigarettes, people, lectures, books, movies – all are consumed, swallowed. The world is one great object for our appetite, a big apple, a big bottle, a big breast; we are the sucklers, the eternally expectant ones, the hopeful ones – and the eternally disappointed ones.'[40] In the West today, writes Terry Eagleton:

> The family remains in part a refuge from civil society, nurturing vital impulses unfulfilled by it; but since it is also ceaselessly penetrated by commodity culture, this potentially positive arena of the personal is continually caught up with forms of privatization which atomize, serialize and disconnect.[41]

Hedges, in his and Joe Sacco's recent *Days of Destruction, Days of Revolt*, follows this up in reminding his readers of the importance debate-framing plays in society:

> Celebrity courtiers, masquerading as journalists, officially anointed experts and specialists, identify our problems and patiently explain the parameters. All who argue outside the imposed parameters are dismissed as irrelevant cranks, extremists, or members of a radical left ... The culture, under the tutelage of these corporate courtiers, becomes a world of

cheerful conformity, as well as an endless and finally fatal optimism. We busy ourselves buying products that promise to change our lives, make us more beautiful, confident, or successful, as we are steadily stripped of rights, money, and influence. All messages we receive through these systems of communication, whether on the nightly news or talks shows like *The Oprah Winfrey Show*, promise a brighter, happier tomorrow.[42]

The influence of celebrities can also shape political attitudes, if only marginally. Physicist Brian Cox and his band 'D:Ream' gained in popularity thanks to a UK Number One hit single of theirs supporting the friendly faces of New Labour in their 1997 campaign, though in early 2010 Cox shifted support to the Liberal Democrats over insufficient science funding. The comedian Eddie Izzard also explained that voting for Labour in 2010 is the right thing to do because their 'heart's in the right place.'[43] Gary Barlow sung similar odes to the Conservatives. In the US, actor Woody Harrelson, a rare outside voice, declared himself an anarchist in the summer of 2013; an important statement if only because the world largely remains one of followers.[44]

Children, now more than ever, are targeted through television and the internet by the public relations industry, leading the CEO of Prism Communications to summarise their innocence in the following terms: 'They aren't children so much as what I like to call "evolving consumers."'[45] Leading people to feel that satisfaction can only be reached through consumption creates a society in which 'around two-thirds of Britons aged between 15 and 35 feel depressed or unhappy at any one time.'[46] In early 2005, the *Guardian* reported:

The vast majority of teenage girls in Britain suffer depression and self-doubt, blaming excessive pressure to look good and succeed in school, according to a poll commissioned by the magazine *Bliss*. Nine out of 10 say they have felt depressed, 42% feel low regularly, and 6% think 'life is not worth living'. They reported feeling pressurised on all fronts: at home, at school and in their social lives. Eighty-four per cent felt burdened with too much homework and coursework at school, and almost two-thirds thought there was too much pressure to succeed academically. Most admitted crying over their homework.[47]

Shevek would surely have none of this, with wage slavery and corporate personhood being just as alien to the anarchist physicist as a demeaning and demoralizing education system. Picking up an economics textbook, 'it bored him past endurance,' reminding him of 'somebody interminably recounting a long and stupid dream.' Like the economists Joseph Stiglitz and Steve Keen, Shevek sees the operations of capitalism as 'the rites of a primitive religion, as barbaric, as elaborate, and as unnecessary.'[48] This is certainly an anarchist nuance of Le Guin's (communism, in contrast, traditionally emphasises industrial efficiency over individual liberty). Similar feelings compel Shevek to explain how on Anarres, in concurrence with Kropotkin's suggestions in *Mutual Aid*, the unwanted and demeaning work on Anarres is equitably distributed, 'unless [an individual] likes the work.'[49] He goes on to explain that this is clearly the only just option: allocating work based on arbitrary school exams will never do for the anarchist. Shevek's loyalty proves to be as strong to Kropotkin as it is to Marx, rejecting the crude assumption of the capitalist that the primary incentive to work is financial, since 'A person likes to do what he is good at doing.'[50] Shevek consequently cites one of the great anarchist thinkers of Anarres, Odo: 'To make a thief, make an owner; to create crime, create laws.'[50] As Hammond also tells the nameless protagonist of *News From Nowhere*, with the abolition of private property and civil law courts, 'Thou shalt not steal had to be translated into, Though shalt work in order to live happily. Is there any need to enforce that commandment by violence?'[52]

On a more philosophical level, the individualist anarchism of Max Stirner (which, it could be argued, is not actually a form of anarchism at all, since it ignores the concerns of the communitarian) seems to suit Shevek best, as we learn during the narrative's account of the protagonist's childhood: 'His heart yearned towards them, the kindly young souls who called him brother, but he could not reach them, nor they him. He was born to be alone, a damned cold intellectual, an egoist.'[53] Winter Elliott seems to concur in his perceptive essay on 'Individual Anarchy,' concluding that the novel is not a blueprint for an anarchist world, but 'a personal utopia, an idea both experienced and realized by one person, Shevek.'[54] But the true anarchist in the novel (certainly by the standards of the Russian and Spanish libertarians) is Shevek's childhood friend, Bedap. After recounting old memories together one night, Bedap identifies a dangerous tendency in human psychology: 'It's always easier not to think for oneself. Find a nice safe hierarchy and settle in. Don't make changes, don't risk disapproval, don't upset your [fellow workers]' (similar themes are explored in Philip K. Dick's provocative short story *The Last of the Masters* and J. M. Coetzee's recent novel *The Childhood of Jesus*).[55] The majority of Anarrestis have forgotten the importance of change and social evolution, leading the planet into a largely passive (though superficially non-hierarchical) cultural and political state, encouraging the rise of authoritarian teachers like Sabul. Consequently, the anarchist planet 'has degenerated into a static society characterized first and foremost by conformity and obedience.'[56] To counter this encroachment, the narrator advises, we should take back the power of socio-political organisation from a group of privileged elites and hand it to the general population, not deluding ourselves into thinking that the modern world's 'complexity' (etc.) requires certain forms of domination and subordination. If one fails to act against forms of illegitimate authority and remain a pampered and pleasured spectator, 'One's freedom to choose and to change will be unused, exactly as if one were in jail.'[57] Thus the goal of the anarchist, like the purpose of the Volunteer Fire Department in Lemony Snicket's *A Series of Unfortunate Events*, is to put out fires and not start them: Shevek vows towards the end of the novel to 'fulfill my proper function in the social organism. I'm going to unbuild walls.'[58] A life lacking such a purpose, as the more recent Snicket would put it, would be one charcterised by asking 'all the wrong questions.'[59]

3

Atheists, Statists, and the English Literati

At one of the numerous deification ceremonies after the death of Christopher Hitchens in December 2011, Stephen Fry described the author and journalist as 'a hero of the mind.' A year earlier, Richard Dawkins had labelled him 'a giant of the mind and a model of courage,' and adoringly chose him as 'my hero of 2010.' Like the historian Simon Schama, Dawkins recently claimed that Hitchens was 'too complex a thinker to be placed on a single left-right dimension. He was a one-off: unclassifiable.' Hitchens was supposedly, like the god of the Christians, beyond comprehension.[1]

While in the process of forming these descriptions, it's quite possible that Fry and Dawkins were reflecting on the time Hitchens told Adam Shatz from the *Nation* that 'If you're actually certain that you're hitting only a concentration of enemy troops [with cluster bombs] ... then it's pretty good because those steel pellets will go straight through somebody and out the other side and through somebody else. And if they're bearing a Koran over their heart, it'll go straight through that, too.' The 2003 invasion of Iraq, and the hundreds of thousands of civilian deaths which predictably followed, were also deemed 'pretty good' by Hitchens. His heroism, then, clearly knew no bounds. One thinks of Achilles.

But these views, though certainly dominant amongst Anglo-American intellectuals, are not shared by the Marxist writer Richard Seymour. Though not quite reaching the level of biography, Seymour's *Unhitched: The Trial of Christopher Hitchens* (attacked upon publication by the 'leftist' *New Statesman* and *Independent*) traces with some detail and subtlety the ideological changes of its boisterous, self-centred, and deceitful antagonist.

Seymour's central argument is that 'not only was Hitchens a man of the right in his last years, but his predilections fr a certain kind of right-wing radicalism ... pre-dated his apostasy.'[2] It is remarkable, and worth discussing briefly, how far the English literary scene is from embracing the anarchist princiles of some of the country's greatest writers (even those which some of its members claim to appreciate, like Orwell). Rather nan working towards social and environmental justice, the le goals and aspirations of a large number of British authors re instead to increase their affluence and readership.

Hitchens's lack of moral principles even led hin to tell Jeremy Paxman in one of his final interviews, around the ame time that he was producing blatantly neoconservative esays on drone warfare, that he still identified himself as par of the left. A minority of journalists pointed out Hitchens's numerous hypocrisies upon his death, and were summarily denounced – as they were after the death of Thatcher – for being disrespectful, malicious, unkind. But as Glenn Greenwald vrote in a *Salon* column shortly after the death of Hitchens, the maxim of 'speak not ill of the death' may apply to personal friends (possibly), but certainly not to public figures, especially the more influential ones.[3]

Hitchens's persistent defence of Rudyard Kpling, his call for 'humanitarian intervention' towards the end of the Gulf War, and his 2007 defence of the Tunisian government ('the most civilised' dictatorship in the Middle East, for him) often lead him to try and justify his contradictory views by calling them 'ironic' or 'dialectical,' cautiously generalising them to avoid rebuttal: He correctly argued that Clinton's bombing of the Al-Shifa pharmaceutical plant was a war crime, but claimed with a straight face that the president was bravely resisting Serbian ultranationalism in Yugoslavia.

Hitchens wasted more time by writing his infamous *Vanity Fair* article 'Why Women Aren't Funny' (with the exception of

those w: ire 'hefty and dykey or Jewish, or some combo of the
three,' l.   eloquently explained). Why exactly he found it
necessary > share this with the world will remain a mystery.
Likewise, s enthusiastic opposition to particular reproductive
rights is (implemented by his social Darwinian praise of the
abortion b nature of 'deformed or idiot children who would
otherwise i ve been born.'[4]

It's quite   ossible, however, as many argue, that Hitchens is
not especi   y worthy of much consideration, so blatantly
contemptib vere his political and journalistic allegiances. But
while it ma   true that he isn't worth thinking about, Hitchens
is certainly   th talking about, not least because of his considerable and vi   ent influence in Britain (especially among young
and relativel   rivileged 'atheists'). Seymour's essay – part of
Verso's *Coun*   *last* series, which aims to 'challenge the apolo-
gists of Empir   and Capital' – should consequently be seen not
just as an expc   ire of 'the Hitch,' but also as a highly valuable
document in tl   continued efforts nationwide to increase the
level of public   litical engagement, countering the temptations
towards stickin   solely to secluded, insular debates about the
problem of evil,   e afterlife, and so on.

In short, anti-   eism often serves to distract from anti-statism
(and anti-corpor   ism), a much more important and urgent
ideological force   The New Atheists, of whom Hitchens was a
principal memb   have always strangely ignored the importance
of politics and   omics in the lives of the devout. Karl Marx,
whose most v   it and repeated writings Hitchens often
obligatorily qu   the same rote monotony of a bored and
distracted A L   'nt, did not:

It is the *tas*   *of* in   re, once the *other-world of truth*
has vanished, to   he *truth of this world*. The
immediate *task of philos*   which is in the service of history,
is to unmask human self-alienation in its *secular form* now that

it has been unmasked in its *sacred form*. Thus the criticism of heaven is transformed into the criticism of earth, the *criticism of religion* into the *criticism of law* and the *criticism of theology* into the *criticism of politics*.[5]

Bertrand Russell mentions in his essay 'An Outline of Intellectual Rubbish' how the dominant state religion of the seventeenth and eighteenth centuries served to keep the disenfranchised population (which they had much distrust of) subordinate and passive, fixating them forever on the glories of the next life which were to be attained through humility and silence. Pierre Corneille proclaimed in 1640 that a respectable citizen should 'Do your duty, and leave the outcome to the Gods.'[6] Like the expressions of profound class hatred found in Luke, Matthew's Gospel similarly demands that we should 'Give to Caesar what is Caesar's, and to God what is God's.'[7]

Even political enfranchisement, when it arrived, was brought about in Britain largely to create the illusion of representation. As F. B. Smith has shown, the reform movement of the 1850s was dominated by the 'incorporation theme':

The radical manufacturing employers were concerned to extend the function of the House because they agreed that if the workingmen were kept outside the electorate, they would come to believe that they held an interest independent of their masters, and would resort to strikes and coercion to gain higher wages and shorter hours.[8]

Complementing the announcement of King Charles I that 'religion is the only firm foundation of power,' before the time of seventeenth-century radicalism and its challenge to the king's divine right, the 'church had evolved a workable system of social control, aided by the useful invention of Purgatory,' with the concept of 'sin' helping to twist an exaggeration of certain innate moral principles into new forms of coercion.[9] These fear-inducing, repressive and morally illegitimate institutions had maintained their influence through to the nineteenth century, as Bakunin explained:

> There is another reason which explains and in some sort justifies the absurd beliefs of the people – namely, the wretched situation to which they find themselves fatally condemned by the economic organization of society in the most civilized countries of Europe. Reduced, intellectually and morally as well as materially, to the minimum of human existence, confined in their life like a prisoner in his prison, without horizon, without outlet, without even a future if we believe the economists, the people would have the singularly narrow souls and blunted instincts of the bourgeois if they did not feels a desire to escape.[10]

Adopting a similar mindset, Alan Sokal recounts his time working in Nicaragua in the mid-1980s alongside Catholics and evangelical Protestants 'whose active solidarity with the poor and downtrodden was inspired by their interpretation of Jesus' teachings. In the face of such exemplary dedication and selfless labor, it would have been churlish of me to draw attention to the irrationality of my friends' supernatural beliefs. Moreover, I had great admiration for those brave Nicaraguans who were ready to risk their lives to protect their fellow citizens from U.S.-organized terrorists; and I realized that in many (but not all) cases, that bravery was bolstered in part by a Christian belief in the afterlife. Of course I thought that belief a delusion, but this in no way lessened my admiration, for I knew that I personally would be much less brave.'[11]

Not sharing Sokal or Bakunin's level of desire for social justice, Stephen Fry's supposedly eloquent and brave defence of the New Atheists in place of those involved in the kinds of anti-authoritarian struggles Sokal describes has often resulted in juvenile outbursts via his favourite medium, Twitter. A few hours after wishing all GCSE candidates good luck in the summer of 2013, during one of his numerous 'conversations' about religion with fellow tweeters Fry claimed sarcastically 'Sure atheists are always setting off bombs, raping women & starting wars in name of non-belief.' His positioning of rape and conflict as exclusively religious pursuits smacks of the kind of intolerance Dawkins often displays, with a number of the famed biologist's Islamophobic tweets generating minor scandals around the same period. Terry Eagleton once made a related observation:

> Novelists such as Salman Rushdie, Martin Amis and Ian McEwan may be vociferous in their opposition to Islamism, but it is hard to imagine any of them speaking out in defence of, say, council workers' wages or the right of Iraqis to defend themselves against a brutal invasion. Given their conditions of labour, writers and artists are unlikely to have much sense of collectivity.[12]

In 2009, Fry and Hitchens were debating partners against Ann Widdecombe and Archbishop John Onaiyekan, debating the usual topic of whether the Catholic Church is a force for good in the world. On August 7th 2013, Fry rightly called on David Cameron and the International Olympic Committee to call a ban on the 2014 Russian Winter Olympics because of Putin's horrific treatment of LGBTs. It was praised universally by the media as 'a masterclass in eloquence,' among other things.[13] But in his melodramatic defence of freedom and justice, he slipped into the usual narrative of defending the 'glorious' corporate organisers behind major sporting events in an effort to, as the IOC puts it, 'cooperate' with 'private organisations and authorities in the endeavour to place sport at the service of humanity and thereby to promote peace' (meaning, allow access to exploitative firms like McDonalds). Fry – the friendly face of Apple – called on Cameron, for whom he has 'the utmost respect,' to carry out the ban of the Winter Olympics whilst simultaneously promoting the commercial forces which not only benefit from it the most, but which also greatly influence state policy. These are presumably the defining features of what he calls 'the civilised world,' a 'glorious' place which 'cannot be seen to have [approved] of' Putin. But as Greenwald puts it, 'I find that Americans and westerners who spend the bulk of their energy on the crimes of others are usually cynically exploiting human rights concerns in service of a much different agenda' – in this case, a naive though well-meaning focus on LGBT issues without giving any thought to the actions of the corporate forces which oppress a far greater range of people.[14]

After publishing his open letter on his website, Fry tweeted a few hours later: 'Oh and in case anyone wants to rape/troll/vilify/beat me up I think Ada Lovelace & Alan Turing should be on next banknote. Computer pioneers.' Humble comments, but what he also seems unaware of is that the man he has the 'utmost respect' for, Cameron, along with a whole host of previous prime ministers, refused to issue an official pardon for the torturous treatment Turing received at the hands of the British state. Turing eventually committed suicide because of it. It was only in July 2013 that backbench MPs managed to force the issue to the government's attention and secure a posthumous pardon.[15] Relatedly, Fry acknowledged in his letter the influence of politics in all aspects of life ('Everyone knows politics interconnects with everything for "politics" is simply the Greek for "to do with the people"'), but didn't seem to grasp the significance of economics and the business interests which shape and inform the state. Ashok Kumar, for instance, pointed out before the 2012 Olympics (which Fry, oddly, had no problem with) that the games have typically been used to restructure the host City at the expense of its working class residents, who are subsequently excluded.[16] Fry's blasé comments on the MPs expenses scandal (forming one of his numerous impressions of his role model Oscar Wilde) also revealed his priorities: style over principle, culture over politics, celebrity over morality. The scandal was 'not that important,' he claimed.[17]

Wilde, an anarchist whose writings are explored below, would not have been impressed. Unless his and other anarchist views are revived, there is little reason to think that Britain will steer away from its current course – propelled by Fry and the stars of *The Apprentice* and *Dragon's Den* – of strengthening pro-business, pro-consumerism 'lifestyles.' These leanings are epitomised by Fry's eager participation in the iPad launch and his starring in numerous TV adverts for friendly products like Orange's 3G and Direct Line's Home Insurance. None of this, of course, is to say that Fry is not an immensely talented figure. In fact it's precisely because his comedic and literary works are so impressive (*A Bit of Fry & Laurie* is one of the smartest and funniest sketch shows Britain has ever produced), and his influence so large, that it becomes more than just annoying when he and other novelists, comedians, and entertainers miss the essential point of John Dewey's remark, that politics, along with the sporting and entertainment events it supports, is largely 'the shadow cast over society by big business.'

What Friedrich Nietzsche (who Hitchens disagreed with for all the wrong reasons) called the Last Man in *Thus Spoke Zarathustra*, described so perceptively by the anarchist sympathiser Chris Hedges in *I Don't Believe in Atheists*, is a label that seems to fit well the philosophy and attitude not only of the New Atheists, but a good deal of western intellectuals more generally:

Nietzsche foresaw the deadening effects of the bourgeois lust for comfort and personal satisfaction. Science and technology might, instead, bring about a race of *Dauermenschen*, of Last

Men. The Last Man would ignore and disdain all that went before him. The Last Man would wallow in his arrogance, ignorance and personal contentment. He would be satisfied with everything he has done. He would seek to become nothing more. He would be stagnant, incapable of growth, part of an easily manipulated crowd. The Last Man would confuse cynicism with knowledge.[18]

In *Unhitched*, Seymour traces the potential for Hitchens to be the author of esteemed columns like 'Why Women Aren't Funny' back to his formative years. He was 'precociously articulate,' reading widely though showing a 'preference early on for literary fiction over, for example, the social sciences, for which it seems probable he had no aptitude.'[19] In his literary criticism, Hitchens abhorred any kind of 'Third Worldism' or 'negritude,' since he was 'unwilling to tolerate the erosion of prestige that such criticism inflicted on the canon.'[20] He even argued in October 1992 that 1492 was 'a very good year' because of the progress in the American colonies which accompanied the genocide of its native population.

Seymour consequently argues that, in his literary and political commentary, Hitchens viewed indigenous life simply as 'raw material' for the ends of 'progressive' colonisation.[21] Echoing points from his brilliantly argued (though poorly titled) *The Liberal Defence of Murder*, Seymour writes that it's of little surprise that Hitchens exploited terms like 'war on terror' and 'humanitarian intervention,' and that when reading essays on Orwell or Paine he 'proved stunningly literal and obtuse, as well as lacking in suppleness when dealing with someone who was too critical of one of his saints.'[22]

All of these attributes echo with some force in Hitchens' writings on religion, for which he is most famous. But Hitchens was at best 'a poor atheist,' for Seymour, making 'secularism seem uninteresting and materialism incondite.'[23] Seymour detects the important role of opportunism in Hitchens' efforts to become a renowned 'antitheist,' observing as he did the popularity of Harris, Dennett and Dawkins. His most celebrated book on religion, which bears the provocative and daring title *God Is Not Great*, 'works as an entertaining expatiation of the sins of imperialism and indeed of capitalism.'[24] He shared with many of the New Atheists the belief that, 'in terms of egregiousness, all religions are equal, and Islam is more equal than others.'[25]

Shamed and disgraced by his politics and journalism, religion became an easy target for Hitchens (and, as Mary Midgley points out, for many 'who do not want to think seriously about the subject'). Lesley Hazleton's perceptive comment captures this well: 'The bulls Hitchens chose were old and lumbering ... so he was never in any danger. Kissinger, long out of power; the wounded Clinton; the pathetically, not-so-sainted Mother Teresa. And of course the most pathetic, lumbering bull of all, God.'[26] David Webster recently stressed that an over-enthusiastic embrace of New Atheism 'may blind us to the many ways that traditional religion might turn out to be an intellectual ally against the laziness of thought and ethical disengagement of the spirituality-movement.' Contemporary spirituality makes us 'stupid, selfish and unhappy,' according to the subtitle of Webster's book *Dispirited*. His reasons are worth quoting:

[T]he inward turn, to the self, to journey on the spiritual quest, often involves a rejection of the mass of detail in the world and a re-evaluation of material, wordly concerns as somehow squalid, shallow and beneath the spiritual aspirant. The sinister consequence, I suggest, of this is that spirituality can be an engine of depoliticisation. There is often a critique within contemporary spirituality of consumerism, seeking happiness in things, and of an unthinking life of sensual self-indulgence. I, like many others, see value in such a critique – but fear that spirituality is a dead-end of a response. It is a response that is a fleeing from these things – not an engagement with them ... Fleeing down an avenue of detachment from the world, we are danger of not only leaving political and social justice behind us, but along with the flight from reason ... there is a danger of descending into a self-regarding and relativistic sentimentality, driven by a solipsistic emotionality.[27]

Focusing on a critique of New Atheism, Seymour claims with ample evidence that Hitchens's argument that 'the worst kind of tyranny ... is religious' carefully distracts his loyal fan base away from state and corporate tyranny – far more dangerous cases, as Hitchens' one-time debating rival, Hedges, so persistently and insightfully points out (in ways which are, incidentally, far more eloquent than Hitchens, allegedly one of the greatest English writers since Orwell).

The New Atheists also carefully set religion an intentionally impossible task (a task only slightly less ludicrous than the claim of many religionists that if science can't explain the origins of the universe with absolute certainty, we should all turn straight to the nearest deity), that 'the Abrahamic religions explain the incompatibility of the Creation story with the findings of contemporary natural and physical sciences.'[28] Hitchens's philosophy of science is at times more absurd than the myths he spent his time debunking, since 'Only by taking a severely reductive and literal approach to the Abrahamic texts, which would be a heterodox view among the religious, can one in all seriousness counterpose the Creation myth to quantum mechanics and find the former at fault for its incompatibility.'[29]

Revealing his Marxist colours, Seymour argues that, by ignoring the social context in which the texts were composed, Hitchens ignores the less obvious fact that – alongside its blood-thirsty tendencies (one anarchist scholar calls Moses 'the Lenin of the pre-Christian world') – the Torah's 'description of the planets and other heavenly bodies, as not personal gods but objects susceptible to physical laws, was a revolutionary idea in its time.'[30] Though it is not at all clear that the notion of 'physical law' would have presented itself to the craftsmen of the Genesis myth, Seymour's indictment of cultural and theological illiteracy on Hitchens' part is nevertheless a highly convincing one.

And where Hitchens claimed that Wycliffe and Coverdale were burned at the stake for their Biblical translations, Seymour cites William Hamblin's observation that the former died of natural causes, while the latter died 'unburned in 1568 at the age of eighty-one.'[31] All of this, of course, is not to 'side' with religion over the New Atheists – Seymour rightly rejects both – it's rather to demonstrate how ignorant and careless Hitchens was in being unable even to construct a coherent and accurate attack on some of history's easiest targets.

Hitchens was also often filmed alongside fellow atheists Dawkins, Sam Harris (another staunch neoconservative, whose writings Glenn Greenwald recently exposed as deeply bigoted), and Daniel Dennett – who together formed the 'Four Horsemen' – discussing with wonder and awe the 'intricate complexity' and 'stunning variety' of the natural world, each of them providing their own view from their respective fields.[32] But since the universe is so beautiful, why is it that the Horsemen largely failed to attend to the concerns of its most remarkable life form? The New Atheist's Islamophobia, for instance, exhibits 'central feature[s] of racism,' for Seymour: 'essentialist thinking, ascriptive denigration, and demonology.'[33]

It is also notable how the New Atheist's hatred of faith schools and Intelligent Design is countered by their promotion of 'rational education,' though their idea of rationality never seems to encompass political or economic education. If a more rational, just and humane world is what they are seriously striving for, then the New Atheists simply have the wrong priorities. Moshe Adler explores in *Economics for the Rest of Us* how, 'Arguably, the damage from the teaching of the economist's theory of wages is far greater than the damage from the teaching of creationism.'[34] The dogmas of neoliberal politics and neoclassical economics are among the most dangerous ideologies in human history. Part of the reason they continue to be taught is because, unlike religion, it is rare that a child or student is emotionally hurt or offended by an economics course. The claim that corporations serve the public good and pay their workers simply what they deserve is much more harmful to society and the natural world than, for instance, the claim that Elijah rode a flaming chariot to heaven.

The thought that people should be unable to discuss openly, organise, or participate in public or economic affairs remains a favoured principle of the modern 'liberal democracy,' demonstrated clearly through clandestine operations and the classification of government documents, as well as through the secrecy and unaccountability of corporate decisions. The modern corporation is today's dominant institution, in many ways like the church or the monarchy in more honest times. They are run by board structures and are hierarchical almost to the purest extent possible, 'persons' with extraordinary wealth and privilege quite far removed from the original corporations during the industrial revolution, which were ephemeral, chartered entities existing explicitly to serve a public good. Bernard Ingham, Thatcher's press spokesman and 'uncivil servant' in the words of the *Independent*, once told American journalists: 'There is no freedom of information in this country; there's no public right to know. There's a commonsense idea of how to run a country and Britain is full of commonsense people ... Bugger the public's right to know. The game is the security of the state – not the public's right to know.'[35] The outgoing Cabinet Secretary Gus O'Donnell essentially concurred with Ingham, telling *The Times* in 2011 that Cabinet should be a 'safe space' for discussion, free from public auspices, and that transparency would lead to less effective government.[36] Similarly, when asked to produce the receipts of

MPs expenses in court, Andrew Walker, director of Parliament's Department of Resources, informed the court that 'MPs should be allowed to carry out their duties free from interference,' and that 'Transparency will damage democracy.'[37]

Gerrard Winstanley, in his 1652 *The Law of Freedom*, seems to have predicted these anti-democratic sensibilities:

> One sort of children shall not be trained up only to book learning and no other employment, called scholars, as they are in the government of monarchy; for then through idleness and exercised wit therein they spend their time to find out policies to advance themselves to be lords and masters above their labouring brethren [sic].[38]

Moreover, as John Gray writes in *Straw Dogs*: 'Humanists like to think they have a rational view of the world; but their belief in progress is a superstition, further from the truth about the human animal than any of the world's religions.'[39] Gray is another 'unclassifiable' political thinker, whose ideas shift from left to right at their author's good pleasure. Some pages later, he shifts to a reactionary, Steven Pinker-esque perspective, claiming that humans are 'weapon-making animals with an unquenchable fondness for killing.'[40] Strictly speaking, this is hard to disagree with when taken literally, but Gray's general lack of appreciation throughout his career for what Kropotkin called 'mutual aid' puts him closer to Hitchens than it does Hedges (who also speaks of the illusions of the humanist belief in 'progress,' but from a Christian anarchist perspective).

Hitchens's irrationality and bigotry was displayed on many other occasions, most notably when he wrote after the November 2004 siege of Fallujah that 'the death toll is not nearly high enough ... too many [jihadists] have escaped,' adding a couple of years later that 'it's a sort of pleasure as well as a duty to kill these people' – one of the reasons why Norman Finkelstein once told me Hitchens is 'worth zero.' With similar compassion, he later spoke of Iran: 'As for that benighted country, I wouldn't shed a tear if it was wiped off the face of this earth.' Indeed, for all his hatred of religion, Hitchens' savage political attitudes often made the Lord of the Old Testament appear fairly soft-hearted.

Rather than uncritically associating Hitchens with the tradition of Reason and the Enlightenment, *Unhitched* intelligently characterises Hitchens' rhetoric as similar to the 'martial discourse that emerged on the right in World War I, was sustained by fascism in the interwar period, and had its consummation in World War II.' To choose one particularly striking example, in July 2007 – still thinking up smart new ways to defend his position on Iraq – Hitchens claimed that the sight of people jumping from the crumbling towers of the World Trade Centre was 'not that terrifying ... That kind of thing happens in a war, it has to be expected in a war ... you should reckon about once a week. Get ready for it.'[41]

After the Iraq War was revealed without any doubt to be an unusually (though predictably) savage catastrophe, Hitchens 'merely fantasised that the Bush administration was the equivalent of the Workers' Party of Marxist Unification, and he was *shocked* to find that they were selling out his just war,' before moving on 'without ever having to really account for what he had done.'[42]

Like the older Aldous Huxley, Hitchens 'esteemed collectivism at least some of the time but never submitted to it himself,' while he also 'resented the rich and powerful but enjoyed their company.'[43] The critiques Hitchens constructed often focused on personality over policy. Even in his early days, he 'had a tendency to revile the personnel of American statecraft without a great deal of emphasis on the structures of power.'[44] He pursued further self-serving policies by emigrating to the US in 1981, where he 'positioned himself as an English radical amid compromising liberals,' attending all the right parties and charming the sleek editors of the glossiest monthlies (the gorgeous Graydon Carter comes to mind).

Hitchens lifted much of the material for his essay 'Kissinger's War Crimes in Indonesia' from Chomsky and Edward Herman's *The Washington Connection and Third World Fascism*, and was later to smear Chomsky, shamefully attack Edward Said, defend the Whitehouse's extrajudicial killing of Anwar al-Awlaki and Osama bin Laden, and praise drone warfare more generally. If further extensive critiques of such dominant literary, political and intellectual figures (Martin Amis, Salman Rushdie, Richard Dawkins, Andrew Marr, Dominic Sandbrook, John Gray, Simon Schama, Niall Ferguson, amongst others) were to arise, and the anarchist worlds, principles and achievements explored by writers like Orwell, Huxley and Morris were to be presented as alternative social visions, then a form of intellectual self-defence against the kinds of chauvinism and moral degeneracy promoted by many secular statists would quickly surface.

4

Workers and Writers

Grown-ups never understand anything by themselves, and it is tiresome for children to be always and forever explaining things to them.
Antoine de Saint Exupéry[1]

Yes, a key can lie forever in the place where the locksmith left it, and never be used to open the lock the master forged it for.
Ludwig Wittgenstein[2]

Recent studies of working class literature have shown convincingly that the novels and diaries of Victorian and pre-industrial workers were just as, and in some cases more, politically insightful and morally astute as the essays of Britain's most esteemed intellectuals. One unusually detailed study, Jonathan Rose's *The Intellectual Life of the British Working Classes*, covers a remarkable range of demanding and urgent questions relevant to the focus of this book. It is notable for its discussion of how writers and academics seek to elevate themselves above the public with unnecessary and exclusionist 'Marxist jargon, modernist obscurantism, or postmodern opacity' – embodying the maxim: if you haven't got anything interesting or original to say, you'd better start flicking through the thesaurus.[3]

Echoing many points from John Carey's *The Intellectuals and the Masses*, Rose makes it clear he is not impressed by most of the literary residues of academic careerism. Modernism comes in for particularly heavy scorn. Indeed, Rose believes 'the fundamental motive behind the modernist movement was a corrosive hostility toward the common reader. Nietzsche, Ortega y Gasset, George Gissing, H. G. Wells, Bernard Shaw, T. S. Eliot, Virginia Woolf,

Sigmund Freud, Aldous Huxley, Wyndham Lewis, D. H. Lawrence, Ezra Pound, and Graham Greene all strove to preserve a sense of class superiority by reviling the mean suburban man.'[4] Woolf, for instance, displaying her enormous snobbery, dismissed *Ulysses* after meeting James Joyce at Hogarth House by calling it 'the book of a self taught working man,' of 'a queasy undergraduate scratching his pimples.'[5]

Modernism, for Rose, was 'a body of literature and art deliberately made too difficult for a general audience,' with prominent intellectuals 'convincing themselves that the typical clerk was subhuman, machinelike, dead inside, a consumer of rubbishy newspapers and canned food.'[6] The result is poems like 'The Waste Land' which, while stylistically bold and elegiac in its nods to past cultures, is unmatched in its patronising faux sympathy for the workers of the 'Unreal City,' where 'Under the brown fog of a winter dawn, / A crowd flowed over London Bridge, so many, / I had not thought death had undone so many.' The racist and anti-Semitic author of the poem, T. S. Eliot, later argued in the 1930s for a dystopic monoculture, in which only his personal Catholic values persisted: 'The population should be homogeneuous: where two or more cultures exist in the same place they are likely to be fiercely self-conscious or both to become adulterate ... [R]easons of race and religion combine to make any large number of free-thinking Jews undesirable.'[7]

Throughout history, exclusionary language has been used by the educated classes to create a sense of legitimate power, often mystical and divine. In ancient Mesopotamia, for instance, 'scribes were a privileged and exclusive caste, and they commonly concluded cuneiform tablets with the epigram "Let the wise instruct the wise, for the ignorant may not see."'[8] When modernism eventually became mass culture, 'the avant-garde had to move on to something more modern still – postmodernism.'[9] Like Alan Sokal and Jean Bricmont's superb exposé *Intellectual Impostures*, Rose explores how 'Latin tags, professional vocabularies, and postmodernist jargon have all been used in turn as forms of encryptions, permitting communication among elites while shutting out everyone else.'[10]

Seeing past the similar oratory of scholars and theologians, the waterman-poet John Taylor satirised how academic rhetoric could increase the prestige of literature by excluding those not privy to the workings of the Ivory Tower:

> Yet I with Non-sense could contingerate,
> And catophiscoes terragrophiocate,
> And make myself admired immediately,
> Of such as understand no more than I.[11]

Seventeenth-century radicals like Taylor and Gerrard Winstanley 'could beat academics at their own game,' the historian Christopher Hill noted, something which has always frightened intellectuals.[12] The labour presses of northern Victorian workers served such a purpose. Around the turn of the twentieth century, Robert Blatchford's *Clarion* reached the masses affordably and presented issues from a socialist perspective in plain language. William Hazlitt, one of the greatest English journalists and a staunch radical, declared that 'more *home* truths are to be learnt from listening to a noisy debate in the alehouse than from attending to a formal one on the House of Commons ... the mass of society have common sense, which the learned in all ages want.'[13]

The popular *Daily Herald* in Britain, to take another example amongst many, lacked advertising support through the late 1960s and eventually had to shut down due to the sparkling advertising banners of competitors. More generally, the independent press survived in Britain up until around the 1970s, at which point it succumbed to concentrations of capital in the 'free market,' and support for vibrant working class movements disappeared from the mainstream. 'Sports' sections, 'business' sections, and 'travel' sections have been present in most newspapers since, but the lack of a 'labour' section plainly reflects the interests and 'values' of advertisers and corporations. Sir Anthony O'Reilly, the former owner of the Independent News & Media Plc (which published the *Independent* until March 2010), announced in his company's annual report for 2004: 'For the advertiser, the newspaper remains the most effective mechanism to convey to the potential consumer the virtue, value, colour and style of any new product, service or offering that he has.'[14]

This is similar to, though less violent than, the fall of the nineteenth century labour press, including William Cobbett's *Political Register*, the *Black Dwarf*, Feargus O'Connor's *Northern Star*, and the *Gorgon*. J. F. C. Harrison has written that 'the strategy of the struggle against the newspaper stamp duties ("taxes on knowledge"), which made papers expensive and therefore beyond the reach of working people, was ... to publish unstamped papers openly and defiantly.' As a result of this insubordination, between 1830 and 1836, over seven hundred people were prosecuted for publishing 'unstamped' newspapers – a heavy blow for any civilised conception of freedom of speech. The corporate press which is praised today as a beacon of liberalism failed to fool the radicals of the 1940s, who dismissed it for 'carefully glossing over the sins of the banking and industrial magnates who really control the nation.'[15]

In his extensive study of the British media, rarely discussed outside academic circles, Raymond Kuhn pointed out in 2007 that 'the importance of advertising as a source of finance and the huge increase in capital investment required for mass publication of newspapers resulted in either the closure of national radical papers, their accommodation to advertising pressure by moving up-market, their confinement to a small ghetto of readers or their acceptance of an alternative source of institutional patronage.'[16] He continues:

Not surprisingly, management attempts to modernize the printing process were fiercely resisted by workers, who sought to protect staff levels and conditions of service. This led to scenes of industrial conflict, first at Eddy Shah's plant in Warrington and then most memorably at Wapping, where Rupert Murdoch's News International had moved in a spectacular entrepreneurial coup in 1986. Backed by the Conservative government's anti-trade union legislation, Murdoch defeated the print workers after a prolonged and sometimes violent dispute.[17]

Working class literature has also proven a fertile ground for radical discussion about other topics, such as education and self-organisation. Thomas Thompson's memoire *Lancashire for Me* is a case in point. 'It was pathetic to see the faith in education as a cure for all ills,' argued Thompson, a member of a workingman's naturalist society who emerged out of the Lancashire mills through co-operative society classes. The workings of other grassroots and awareness-raising groups in hundreds of chapels and thousands of kitchens became known as 'mutual improvement' (a term used as far back as 1731). Although rarely mentioned in labour history studies, a Coventry millworker once claimed that 'The Labour movement grew out of Mutual Improvement Societies.'[18] In 1817 Robert Owen proposed that capitalism should be replaced by self-managed communities based on principles of free association, and in 1821 a socialist community was established at Spa Fields, lasting until 1824. Other co-operative societies emerged alongside mutual improvement clubs.

Taking the role of the managerial class into account, Daniel and Gabriel Cohn-Bendit pointed out in *Obsolete Communism* that 'A society without exploitation is inconceivable where the management of production is controlled by one social class, in other words where the division of society into managers and workers is not totally abolished.'[19] The French anarchist Pierre-Joseph Proudhon's method of making the exploitative nature of the manager-worker relation more clear was to distinguish between 'ownership,' which he saw as feudal, and 'possession,' which he saw as egalitarian and synonymous with workers' control over production. Property would consequently be replaced by joint ownership on the part of the producers ('possessors'), united in federal cooperation. In typical anarchist fashion, Orwell likewise maintained in a letter written a year before his death that 'The real division is not between conservatives and revolutionaries but between authoritarians and libertarians.'[20]

As with these anarchist attitudes towards employment, the suspicion towards the wonders of 'education' exhibited by the above writers survived through to the workers of later centuries, with the schools of the early 1900s imposing a 'desiccated diet of irrelevant facts' according to the educational historian H. C. Dent, where students were tasked with regurgitating conventional pieties and memorising equations.[21] The disciplines of today largely stay true to this conception of Knowledge, with AQA's recent history textbook on *The Making of Modern Britain* – full of exciting exercises to test your source-reading skills! – carefully side-stepping the more embarrassing aspects of the nation's foreign exploits. John Dewey, in his classic *Experience and Education*, despised with Dent the 'diet of predigested materials' students are typically forced to follow:

> What avail is it to win prescribed amounts of information about geography and history, to win ability to read and write, if in the process the individual loses his own soul: loses his appreciation of things worth while, of the values in which these things are relative; if he loses desire to apply what he has learned and, above all, loses the ability to extract meaning from his future experiences as they occur?[22]

Defending a less mechanical and tedious lifestyle, one particular biology tutor from Leeds at the Workers' Educational Association condemned the 'stamp collecting' method of science education: 'To merely lecture the students that offer themselves, or to get them to read books is to produce nothing but inflation and arrogance.'[23] Sharing similar libertarian roots, the students of the WEA cited intellectual independence as a prime goal of education, as the 1936 Williams-Heath survey discovered. One student believed education exists 'To enable a man to stand on his own feet. To equip him to be able to endure his own company on occasions, communing with the inner world of his thoughts, instead of rushing out to mix with the crowd.'[24]

Though it's no doubt less oppressive than in Victorian times, the education system in contemporary Britain still selects for obedience and conformity, with the students who are willing to do every pointless homework assignment being handed certificates on prize giving day before moving onto university, where the same values of deference are encouraged. The American pioneer of homeschooling, John Holt, also spent a great deal of effort trying to liberate education from its role as a state apparatus (we're wandering into Louis Althusser's terminology here – careful!) whose primary use is coaching obedience and subordination:

Education ... now seems to me perhaps the most authoritarian and dangerous of all the social inventions of mankind. It is the deepest foundation of the modern slave state, in which most people feel themselves to be nothing but producers, consumers, spectators, and 'fans', driven more and more, in all parts of their lives, by greed, envy, and fear. My concern is not to improve 'education' but to do away with it, to end the ugly and antihuman business of people-shaping and to allow and help people to shape themselves.

Holt wrote elsewhere in *How Children Fail* that 'The anxiety children feel at constantly being tested, their fear of failure, punishment, and disgrace, severely reduces their ability both to perceive and to remember, and drives them away from the material being studied into strategies for fooling teachers into thinking they know what they really don't know.'[25]

In his extensive and articulate study of *Science and Education*, Thomas Huxley described in 1868 what he saw as the most humane goal any decent education should strive towards:

> That man, I think, has had a liberal education who has been so trained in youth that his body is the ready servant of his will, as does with ease and pleasure all the work that, as a mechanism, it is capable of; whose intellect is a clear, cold, logic engine, with all its parts of equal strength, and in smooth working order; ready, like a steam engine, to be turned to any kind of work, and spin the gossamers as well as forge the anchors of the mind; whose mind is stored with a knowledge of the great and fundamental truths of Nature and of the laws of her operations; one who, no stunted ascetic, is full of life and fire, but whose passions are trained to come to heel by a vigorous will, the server of a tender conscience; who has learned to love all beauty, whether of Nature or of art, to hate all vileness, and to respect others as himself.[26]

The primary schools of Huxley's time taught children a 'certain amount of regularity, attentive obedience, respect for others: obtained by fear, if the master be incompetent or foolish; by love and reverence, if he be wise.'[27] Even the subject of university education he thought 'awful,' and 'one I almost fear to touch with my unhallowed hands.'[28] His basic assumption was that any school system which is geared towards test-passing is inevitably going to fall into great difficulty. Noam Chomsky's father, William, defined one of the main objectives of his life as 'the education of individuals who are well integrated, free and independent in their thinking, concerned about improving and enhancing the world, and eager to participate in making life more meaningful and worthwhile for all.'[29] In his *Proposed Roads to Freedom*, Russell also outlined what he thought to be the correct approach to human affairs and social relations:

> Those whose lives are fruitful to themselves, to their friends, or to the world are inspired by hope and sustained by joy: they see in imagination the things that might be and the way in which they are to be brought into existence. In their private relations they are not preoccupied with anxiety lest they should lose such affection and respect as they receive: they are engaged in giving affection and respect freely, and the reward comes of itself without their seeking. In their work they are not haunted by jealousy of competitors, but are concerned with the actual matter that has to be done. In politics, they do not spend time and passion defending unjust privileges of their class or nation, but they aim at making the world as a whole happier, less cruel, less full of conflict between rival greeds, and more full of human beings whose growth has not been dwarfed and stunted by oppression.[30]

Like Russell and Huxley, the Cartesians and classical liberals believed that the defining feature of humanity is freedom. The development of classical liberalism into later varieties of libertarian socialism has led one anti-neoliberal activist to define anarchism as 'liberalism on steroids.'[31] All of the above writers, and many more besides, would have consequently found it hard to side with Britain's Secretary of State for Education, Michael Gove, and his competition-oriented and business-friendly approach to schooling. They would have likely sided instead with Isaac Newton, who defined his critical spirit in the following terms: 'I don't know what I may seem to the world, but as to myself, I seem to have been only like a boy playing on the sea-shore and diverting myself in now and then finding a smoother pebble or a prettier shell than ordinary, whilst the great ocean of truth lay all undiscovered before me.'[32] In Britain, 'academies' can today be sponsored by virtually anyone, and the government has wholeheartedly embraced the notion of banks doing so, helping entrench an already dominant corporate philosophy of 'motivation' into schools. One teacher informed Stephen Bayley at the *Guardian* that 'we do Napoleon' to learn History and French, with a bonus being that pupils 'learn about motivational leadership.'[33] Even senior examiners and business leaders have condemned the industrial legacy of the 'exam factory' approach for 'damaging education.' One of its consequences was felt in August 2013 when GCSE results declined by a record margin, partly because of the 'perverse incentives' waved at teachers and headteachers in the form of league tables; partly also because, as Dewey noted, educational institutions will never succeed in their official goals so long as 'only the textbook and teacher have a say ... every individual becomes educated only as he has an opportunity to contribute something from his own experience, no matter how meager or slender that background of experience may be at a given time.'[34]

The former Professor of English Literature at Manchester University, Terry Eagleton, summarises his experience by writing that, 'By and large, academic institutions have shifted from being the accusers of corporate capitalism to being its accomplices. They are intellectual Tescos, churning out a commodity known as graduates rather than greengroceries.'[35] In Spring 2011, Morrisons announced it intended to fund business degrees at Bradford University, intensifying Eagleton's imagery. Intensifying it even more, in his study of critical discourse analysis, Norman Fairclough studied an extract from a university prospectus and demonstrated how the text's language presents students as consumers and education as a product to be marketed like any product sold in supermarkets.[36]

Given this background, it's worth considering what the increasingly symbolic appointments of university chancellors and their ceremonial role reveals about the nature of Britain's universities, and their reliance on corporate power, with the wealth of Britain's three major political parties being largely the result of donations from financial, arms, commercial and pharmaceutical interests. As Owen Hatherley depicts in his commendably broad and disturbing *A Guide to the New Ruins of Great Britain*, the University of Nottingham's Jubilee Campus 'begs the viewer (and this is *viewing* architecture, not something physical) to applaud its vaulting geometries, bids us be dazzled by its colour scheme, to the point where a violent reaction is all but inevitable. This is, in function as much as in form, the ideal neoliberal university, made up of "business incubator units" and "fitness suites".'[37] In the spirit of handing post-industrial cities over to tourism and the 'creative industries,' in Nottingham the 'monuments to industrial power and civic pride are now more often housing bars, shops, "number 1 Eighties Nights" and seventies theme pubs. In one example of sheer historical farce, a Pitcher and Piano inhabits a former Unitarian church,' a potent symbol of the neoliberal opiate of personal pleasure and consumption.[38] Likewise, Manchester's 'People's History Museum' is built inside the city's Business Quarter, 'as if to quarantine the city's radical past on site.'[39]

In Merseyside, the Liverpool ONE shopping zone is 'a privatized city-district where public rights of way [are] irrelevant, an enclave shutting itself off and boasting its own private security force and a policy of keeping undesirables of its streets.'[40] It is intended not for scousers from Everton or Bootle, but purely for wealthier 'Liverpudlians' from Cheshire, Woolton, Halewood, and other enclaves of middle class individualism. It is a place 'where civic virtues are secondary to the imperative of spend spend spend,' Hatherley rightly observes.[41] Children in Liverpool no longer grow up near useful, productive industries, but live next door to shopping centres and retail 'parks,' encouraging them to mindlessly consume and not think to use their creative and intellectual faculties for anything but to strategically purchase the latest offers. A few miles away, at Stanley Dock, there are huge monuments of Merseyside's industrial legacy surrounding caravan homes. It is a place where 'an old idea of urbanism is utterly ruined ... and you can smell its decomposition. Yet it feels so much less ruinous than the desolate city of property and tourism just a couple of miles away.'[42]

The piazzas of Italy, on the other hand, with their communal fountains and park spaces, all reveal anarchist tendencies of solidarity. Alternatively, take the typical Japanese house, 'essentially one big room, divided by sliding screens as desired, for the activity of life is ever varying. Outside and inside are also open to one another.'[43] Kropotkin believed medieval architecture, though religious in tone, was focused on and crucially shaped by its community and inhabitants. The 'functional' or purpose-based architecture of the modern world has unsurprisingly sickened many leftists, one of the most prominent being the distinguished geographer David Harvey:

Even the incoherent, bland and monotonous suburban tract development that continues to dominate in many areas now gets its antidote in a 'new urbanism' movement that touts the sale of community and boutique lifestyles to fulfill urban dreams. This is a world in which the neoliberal ethic of intense possessive individualism, and its cognate of political withdrawal from collective forms of action, becomes the template for human socialization.[44]

The modern corporation is a major tool in the hands of neoliberal politicians used to build this kind of world. To briefly return to Nottingham, in October 2012 it was revealed that the CEO of

GlaxoSmithKline, Sir Andrew Witty, was to become the University of Nottingham's next Chancellor, an announcement reported with much awe and enthusiasm by local journals.[45] The following January he officially assumed his position. Vice-Chancellor David Greenaway set the tone of discussion by declaring that Witty will 'bring new perspectives to the leadership of our University.' Greenaway saw Nottingham 'going from strength to strength given his vision and commitment,' with the new Chancellor being an 'inspiring' figure ensuring the university's continued 'excellence.'

GlaxoSmithKline is one of the world's largest pharmaceutical corporations, taking on more chemistry graduates from the university than any other firm. In April 2012 it gave Nottingham £12m towards a new sustainable chemistry laboratory due to open in 2014 (described as a generous 'gift' by *This is Nottingham*). But as a corporation, GSK is legally obliged to maximise profits for shareholders, and 'must always put their corporation's best interests first and not act out of concern for anyone or anything else (unless the expression of such concern can somehow be justified as advancing the corporation's own interests),' as the Canadian lawyer Joel Bakan points out in *The Corporation*.[46] CEOs, investors and banks are allowed to co-operate and work together with wealthy states (often referred to as 'democracy'). Workers, however, are not supposed to organise or help one another, but merely compete. Along with GSK, the giant tobacco firm ABT also donated $7 million to the university to create an International Centre for Corporate Social Responsibility, which has led to the creation of satirically-named degrees like 'Corporate Social Responsibility' and so on.

Efforts to protect the environment against harmful pollutants, then, will only be considered if such measures increase the company's market share, with 'the pathological pursuit of profit' (as Bakan rightly calls it) continuing until the legal powers corporations have slowly gained since the nineteenth century are dismantled or undermined.

On July 2nd 2012, GSK pleaded guilty to criminal charges and agreed to pay a $3 billion settlement in the largest health-care fraud case in US history. GSK's achievements include the company's illegal promotion of prescription drugs, bribing doctors, promoting the use of medicines for certain unlicensed uses, and its failure to report safety data. Scrupulously pursuing its legal duty of profit maximisation, throughout the late 1990s and early 2000s (during which it also made a safe $27.5 million from only three antidepressants) GSK issued, for instance, 32,000 secretly ineffective paroxetine prescriptions to children – with the added 'gift' of side-effects like nausea, insomnia and high blood pressure, responses unreported by GSK to doctors, patients, and even regulators. The fifth edition of the *Diagnostic and Statistical Manual of Mental Disorders*, released in May 2013, has also hugely expanded the range of what are considered mental illnesses, which now include teenage rebelliousness, opening the door for Big Pharma to prescribe even more psychiatric 'remedies.'[47]

The lack of any criminal charges for executives (as with the 'banksters' who are 'too big to jail' after the Great Recession, such as Matt Ridley of Northern Rock, a staunch neoliberal advocate) would have been of little surprise to the seventeenth-century jurist Sir Edward Coke, who complained that companies 'cannot commit treason, nor be outlawed, nor excommunicated, for they have no souls.'[48] For the 'morally blind' corporation, Bakan adds, human beings are merely (though strictly) 'tools to generate as much profit as possible.'[49] It is of little surprise that GSK was charged with 'showering doctors with gifts, consulting contracts, speaking fees, even tickets to sporting events' to increase sales of prescription drugs, according to a careful and perceptive *Salon* essay by Robert Reich.[50] Despite this, the University of Nottingham's website repeatedly insists with unusual generosity that GSK is 'committed to improving the quality of human life by enabling people to do more, feel better and live longer.'

The heads of higher education institutions are not the only influential figures to ignore the effects of converting education into a business. Probably the most respected man in Britain, Sir David Attenborough, upon receiving an Honorary Degree from the University of Leicester claimed at its 2006 graduation ceremony that 'A university is an important, crucial, vital element in a city because it is one of the very few institutions in our community which is affected in its teaching, and in its research, and in its thought not by commercial interests, not by political pressure, but by a care for what is true.'[51]

Today, many anarchists see the state as the highest form of oppression in society. But this is surely no longer the case. As Noam Chomsky has pointed out, the characteristic of the state which most frightens corporate elites is its potential to be partially democratic (through the franchise and representative accountability). Enticed by the 'natural entity' view of corporations, it is easy to forget that they are wholly dependent on the state and judicial system for their creation and subsequent power. Corporations are therefore an offshoot of state power; a 'Frankenstein monster' for Supreme Court Justice Louis Brandeis. James Wilson believes 'State authority is justified when it prevents autocratic authority that is not responsible to the populace and subsequently overwhelms the populace's autonomy and capacity to freely and fully associate with one another.' We should

continually evaluate a government and other forms of institutional authority by asking such empirical questions as: how decently does the institution treat each individual member (including those 'aliens' unofficially affiliated but nevertheless profoundly affected by that society)? How are wealth and power distributed? How much choice do all people have in pursuing their chosen goals? How monotonous is their work?

Which of those individuals subject to the institution have meaningful, adequate rights that protect them from violence and from private and/or state tyranny?[52]

In spite of what their name would suggest, the anarchists have typically stressed that the real enemy of a free humanity is not necessarily the state, but the private concentrations of power which have operated coercively throughout the centuries. Indeed, the bulk of working class activists, socialists and anarchists in late nineteenth-century Britain believed that effective democratic change without a revolution would be impossible until the efforts of strikers and protestors (and political opportunism) brought Gladstone's government around to extending the franchise to two-thirds of the adult male population in 1884. But the notion of the public taking direct control of their lives was too much for Gladstone to bear, and writing in the *Nineteenth Century* in 1878 he confessed that the few must always be ruled by the many: 'It is written in legible characters, and with a pen of iron, on the rock of human destiny, that within the domain of practical politics the people must in the main be passive.'[53]

In the current world economy, the state provides some form of self-defence against corporate tyranny, ultimately to be dismantled in the long term (since, as Oscar Wilde complained, it was not satisfactory to live in a world of charity, but rather in a world in which charity is unnecessary). Working towards this requires solving problems under our immediate influence. In this sense the nationalisation of certain banks, for example, is of greater benefit both to democratic organization and to the domestic economy than bailing them out. Once the bank is nationalised, decisions can be made as to how it's run: Is it run by the community, or by a select group of academically qualified 'experts'? On this crucial topic of decentralisation, Rudolf Rocker had this to say:

For the state centralisation is the appropriate form of organisation, since it aims at the greatest possible uniformity in social life for the maintenance of political and social equilibrium. But for a movement whose very existence depends on prompt action at any favourable moment and on the independent thought and action of its supporters, centralism could but be a curse by weakening its power of decision and systematically repressing all immediate action ... Organisation is, after all, only a means to an end. When it becomes an end in itself, it kills the spirit and the vital initiative of its members and sets up that domination by mediocrity which is the characteristic of all bureaucracies.[54]

These decentralising and libertarian tendencies have been noted in the past by eminent figures, quite often to denounce them. The liberal Whig historian Thomas Babington Macaulay thought that 'Universal suffrage would be fatal for all purposes for which government exists,' since it was thought to be 'incompatible with the existence of capitalism.'[55] Another 'liberal' journal, the Social Darwinian *Economist*, in 1846 had 'no hesitation in pronouncing, because the masses are suffering, and have long been suffering, without must amending their condition, that they are greatly to blame ... Nature makes them responsible for their conduct – why should not we?'[56] Just over a hundred years later, Richard Crossman wrote that the leaders of British society 'profoundly distrust active democracy.'[57] When we go further to the right, the great man of letters, Samuel Johnson, wrote in 1773 that the definition of a good government is one in which 'the wise see for the simple, and the regular act for the capricious.'[58] Tory luminaries accordingly feared the 'disaster of democracy' after Disraeli's skillful passing of the 1867 Reform Act, and after the 1884 Reform Act William Harcourt, Gladstone's Home Secretary, announced that the bill was a 'frightfully democratic measure which I confess appals me.'[59] Here is Chomsky's view on indoctrination and state dogma from an interview with David Barsamian in October 1986:

> [T]here's been a very sharp decline since the Middle Ages. In the Middle Ages, when you read Thomas Aquinas, he felt that he had to deal with heresy. He wanted to defend the doctrines of the faith against heresy, but he felt he had to understand it. Medieval theology was an honest intellectual atmosphere: if people had heretical arguments you had to pay attention to them, think about them, find answers to them. We've degenerated far below that in modern culture. Here you don't have to understand heresy, you just point to it, you just say, 'Look, this guy's involved in heresy,' and that's the end of that discussion.[60]

Unlike the above reformist measures, the notion of a spontaneous or even well-planned revolution has, like all rebellions, potential for violence and corruption; there will always be Lenins, attention-grabbers and ego-trippers among activists who feel the need to sideline the views of others and control their group's activities. People will always ask, like George Scialabba, 'How many damn meetings would we all have to go to?'[61] And for Orwell, 'Most revolutionaries are potential Tories, because they imagine that everything can be put right by altering the *shape* of society; once that change is effected, as it sometimes is, they see no need for any other.'[62] Kropotkin replies to these concerns: 'We do not deny that there are plenty of egotistic instincts in isolated individuals. We are quite aware of it. But we contend that the very way to revive and nourish these instincts would be to confine such questions ... to any board or committee, in fact, to the tender mercies of officialism in any shape or form. Then indeed all the evil passions spring up, and it becomes a case of who is the most influential person on the board.'[63] Kropotkin consequently denounced the small number of self-labelled anarchists who terrorised Europe during the later decades of the nineteenth century, warning against 'the illusion that one can defeat the coalition of exploiters with a few pounds of explosives.'[64]

The relationship between principle and practice many political thinkers have written about is constantly on the mind of any politically or ideologically motivated movement, and anarchism has been no exception. Though his attack was focused more on anarchist writers like Hakim Bey and John Zerzan, Murray Bookchin's infamous criticism of what he called 'lifestyle anarchism' in 1995 maintains a certain degree of relevance today (though he seems to suggest there are 'right' and 'wrong' ways to be an anarchist). Any serious anarchist committed to notions of creativity and free speech should welcome alternative lifestyles, modes of dress, new foods and so on, but not at the expense of anti-authoritarian actions. Indeed, they can often work in tandem. We might also argue in favour of what Bookchin calls the polar opposite of 'lifestyle anarchism,' namely 'social anarchism' (what he, perhaps aggressively, sees as 'real' anarchism), so long as it doesn't do away with or diminish the essential importance of lifestyle changes. Bookchin writes in *Social Anarchism or Lifestyle Anarchism: An Unbridgeable Chasm?*:

The 1990s are awash in self-styled anarchists who – their flamboyant radical rhetoric aside – are cultivating a latter-day anarcho-individualism that I will call lifestyle anarchism. Its preoccupations with the ego and its uniqueness and its polymorphous concepts of resistance are steadily eroding the socialistic character of the libertarian tradition ... Ad hoc adventurism, personal bravura, an aversion to theory oddly akin to the antirational biases of postmodernism, celebrations of theoretical incoherence (pluralism), a basically apolitical and anti-organizational commitment to imagination, desire, and ecstasy, and an intensely self-oriented enchantment of everyday life ... a state of mind that arrogantly derides structure, organization, and public involvement; and a playground for juvenile antics.[65]

Lacking the risk of revolutionary and counter-revolutionary violence are libertarian socialist reforms, such as those carried out under the Rehn-Meidner plan in 1970s Sweden, which offered to gradually buy shares from the owners of businesses to convert the nation into a worker-owned democracy. A 20% tax on corporate profits would go to union-controlled wage earner funds, which would then be reinvested in the firm. But in the mid-1970s the Swedish Employers' Federation saw a surge in membership and persuasively preached anti-tax, anti-welfare neoliberal doctrines. When the Conservative government later opted to join the EU in 1993-4, Sweden was forced by this neoliberal agenda to focus on deficit reduction and inflation control instead of full employment, social equality, human, animal and environmental rights, and so forth. These policies of maintaining low wages and concentrating wealth and poverty are not mere by-products of neoliberalism, as economists like Stiglitz hold, but are 'the fundamental core of what neoliberalisation has been about all along.'[66]

For these reasons we can perhaps sympathise with the Christian anarchists, a tradition Leo Tolstoy popularised, though which diminished considerably over the last century:

The revolutionaries say: 'The government organization is bad in this and that respect. It must be destroyed by this and that.' But a Christian says: 'I know nothing about the governmental organization or in how far it is good or bad, and for that reason I do not wish to overthrow it, but for the same reason I do not want to support it. And I not only do not want to, but I cannot, because what it demands of me is against my conscience.'[67]

The corporate principles Joel Bakan and others denounce, of legal constructions being accorded rights above those of ordinary people, derive from the English concept of limited liability whereby the owners and investors of a company are not liable or accountable for their actions if sued, and the plaintiffs are instead forced to sue the company. The seventeenth-century philosopher and Cambridge Platonist, Ralph Cudworth, would not have been impressed by this, approving instead of the common sense rarely applied today by respected intellectuals to the concerns of domestic or international affairs – namely, that we should take responsibility for our actions. He wrote that 'necessity is not intrinsic to the nature of every thing, but that men have such a liberty or power over their own actions, as may render them accountable for the same, and blameworthy when they do amiss.'[68] Talk of freedom in a society dominated by corporations is plainly absurd; the only 'freedoms' granted are the rights to rent yourself to them by getting a job or to buy, if you like, whatever it is they sell. Danny Dorling paints a stark picture of this world:

> My surest prediction for the future is that in less than a century's time people will look back at the start of the twenty-first century and ask why those we put in power were callous and mean-spirited, and why we did not do more to stop them from being so.[69]

Bakan notes that corporate 'persons' are legally obliged to subordinate all concerns to the pursuit of profit:

> The law forbids any motivation for their actions, whether to assist workers, improve the environment, or help consumers save money. They can do these things with their own money, as private citizens. As corporate officials, however, stewards of other people's money, they have no legal authority to

pursue such goals as ends in themselves – only as means to serve the corporation's own interests, which generally means to maximise the wealth of its shareholders. Corporate social responsibility is thus illegal – at least when it is genuine.[70]

This makes an absurdity, to say the least, out of Ed Miliband's belief in 'responsible capitalism.' As in neoliberal Chile, Taiwan, Singapore and South Korea, the ease with which authoritarian politics combines with state capitalist economics should give us pause when David Cameron and George Osborne speak of capitalism being essential to democracy. The legal obligation firms have to pursue profit at the expense of all else is depicted well in Paul Thomas Anderson's remarkable film *There Will Be Blood*, set in the hills and deserts of California in the early decades of the twentieth century. Daniel Day-Lewis plays the part of Daniel Plainview (putting on what some critics have called the greatest male performance since cinema began), a self-proclaimed 'oil man' and 'family man' who sacrifices the livelihood of a small town, along with the childhood of a dead worker's son who he forces to pose as his adorable business partner, in an effort to secure oil. At one point, Plainview, who represents – among other things – corporate personhood and some of the darker aspects of human psychology, explains what Bakan would call his pathological motives:

> I have a competition in me. I want no one else to succeed. I hate most people ... There are times when I look at people and I see nothing worth liking. I want to earn enough money that I can get away from everyone.[71]

In Anderson's next film, *The Master*, set in the post-war American south, Lancaster Dodd, played by the brilliant Philip Seymour Hoffman, takes a slightly different approach to bringing every aspect of his life's work under his control, creating a religious cult in which he alone sets the rules and agenda. In many ways the film presents this as a desperate cry for help in a time when the post-war promises of prosperity began to disintegrate. Dodd tells Joaquin Phoenix's character Freddie Quell in the penultimate scene: 'If you figure a way to live without serving a master, any master, then let the rest of us know, will you? For you'd be the first person in the history of the world [sic].'[72]

It is hoped by British elites that Cameron's attack on public education will discourage such rejection of the infamous Master/Slave relation, and act as disciplinary techniques for the population, who will be forced to work longer and harder to maintain a decent standard of living. Treating students like customers, the Conservative/Liberal Democrat programme aims to market student debt as 'deferred payments' through a conversion of universities into centres of consumerism. Continuing New Labour's effort to make 'education' synonymous with 'competition,' the National Student Survey is based purely on American perspectives on 'customer satisfaction' in universities.[73] Funding for the Arts and Humanities subjects has already been cut, and only the 'priority' disciplines like technology and the sciences will receive (decreased) support – even the Royal Society has predicted 'game over for British science.'[74] Very few vice-chancellors have spoken out against the 'reforms,' leading one ex-VC to announce: 'Whatever view you take of the planned privatization of higher education, it [the silence of VCs] was not a stirring call to arms.'[75]

Along with political leaders and corporate executives, the chancellors and heads of higher education institutions represent a system which promotes conformity and hierarchy, whose symbolic role survives not because of natural law, but because of continued passivity (the easy option), existing merely as a historical residue; or to borrow Russell's description of causality, it is 'a relic of a bygone age, surviving, like the monarchy, only because it is erroneously supposed to do no harm.'[76]

Proceeding to find alternatives, we find that, strictly speaking, there has been no such thing as an 'anarchist school'; there have only been, as Colin Ward once told Judith Suissa, 'different kinds of educational experiments which anarchists have supported and been involved in.'[77] One such highly successful experiment was Fransisco Ferrer's Escuela Moderna, opened in Barcelona in September 1901. The school had 126 pupils enrolled by 1905. In the school's prospectus, Ferrer wrote: 'I will teach them only the simple truth. I will not ram a dogma into their heads. I will not conceal from them one iota of fact. I will teach them not what to think but how to think.'[78] A unique aspect of the school, adhering to the wishes of Wilde and Powys, was its lack of punishment and grades and prizes:

> Having admitted and practiced the coeducation of boys and girls, of rich and poor – having, this is to say, started from the principle of solidarity and equality – we are not prepared to create a new inequality. Hence in the Modern School there will be no rewards and punishments; there will be no examinations to puff up some children with the flattering title of 'excellent', to give others the vulgar title of 'good', and make others unhappy with a consciousness of incapacity and failure.[79]

Ferrer observed that, though they had initially hesitated, the parents of the schools' pupils accepted this anarchist approach, appreciating how 'the rituals and accompanying solemnities of conventional examinations in schools' only served the purpose 'of satisfying the vanity of parents and the selfish interests of many teachers, and in order to put the children to torture before the exam and make them ill afterwards.'[80] The school favoured practical learning through trips to museums, factories and laboratories, though it also embraced scholarly study while remaining suspicious of over-intellectualising topics.

Colin Ward's stress that the very notion of an 'anarchist society' is by definition too inflexible and rigid, implying as it does a fixed set of guidelines for social revolution, is particularly pertinent for anyone concerned with education.[81] In January 1917, the anarchist poet Herbert Read wrote to a friend on the state-anarchy disparity, echoing these concerns:

> I've a theory that all the evil things in the world are static, passive and possessive; and that all good things are dynamic, creative. Life is dynamic: death is static. And as life is dynamic, passive remedies of society are false. Hence the folly of having cut and dried Utopias as ultimate aims: by the time you get to them, life has left them behind. Hence the folly of basing society on possessive institutions (such as property and marriage, as a rule). Our institutions should appeal to our creative impulses: what a man *does* and not what he *has*.[82]

Ken Robinson has pointed out in three illuminating TED talks and a series of compelling books that children are not frightened of bring wrong; a trait which is soon forced out of them through the heightened self-consciousness and anxiety imposed on them through the Anglo-American religious devotion to formal examination and a surreal level of obedience.[83] Robinson claims that a process of 'academic inflation' is occurring whereby grades and degrees are worth far less today than were a generation ago, with the increased 'flexibility' of labour playing a major role (along with the lack of secure tenures, abolished under Thatcher). Sociologist Michael Young shrewdly comments that 'Today you have to be far smarter to get by, and if you are not, we penalize your children.'[84] Indeed, while the government continues to claim proudly that A and A* grades are increasing, a study by Durham University revealed that those exact results would have achieved a C grade two decades ago.[85]

Relating to Robinson's concerns, there is a revealing body of work by David Hay and his colleague Rebecca Nye which document their examinations of children's reactions to real-world situations. They have shown that, during the filtering process of formal education, as children grow older they use less and less words to do with awe and joy to describe features of the world. Hay and Nye have suggested that this is a result of education forcing children out of their creative capacities, rather than helping them grow into them.[86]

Raised in a Catholic crafting family in the Grampians, Anne Kynoch also resented her time at Catholic School and the very existence of the syllabus: 'Despite being reverent and submissive there was still an intense longing to select my own reading, a longing that could not be quenched or denied.'[87] Putting neoliberal Britain's bureaucratised and hierarchical educational world to shame, 'The Sheffield People's College, founded in 1842, was governed democratically by its students: in 1849 the president was a shoemaker. The College taught geography, history, modern languages, Latin, Greek, science, and philosophy, and students were encouraged to discuss politics.'[88] In 2001, the primary school headteacher Peter Stevenson attempted to revive this level of political engagement, and created a controversy after urging teachers at his school to discuss the invasion of Afghanistan.

The breakdown of social barriers through the arts encouraged by the Sheffield People's College was also supported by a variety of progressive corporations (decades before the financialisation of the British economy), with Lyons Teashops, Rowntree's and Cadbury sponsoring a number of drama societies across England. His works not being confined to the theatre, Shakespeare also 'provided a language of radical political mobilization' for many workers, with caravans of barnstorming actors bringing the bard's plays to mining villages across England.[89] In drama classes, 'We were encouraged to think for ourselves,' wrote the cotton mill worker and factory clerk J. R.

Gregson, since knowledge is only of value when 'acquired as a by-product of one's own originality and special turn of mind.'

Industrial drudgery, on the other hand, engendered 'mental apathy' and a 'crippled spirit': 'I have spent my life fighting against this state of mind and temper,' added Gregson, 'both in myself and in my fellows. The working-man's first instinct is to distrust beauty when he is made to see it. Talk to him of what life means to you, and he will confide to his neighbour – behind your back – that you are a bit funny sometimes!'[90]

With similar beliefs outlined and further memoires cited, Rose explores in *The Intellectual Life of the British Working Classes* what he sees as a centuries-old conflict between the educated and self-educated classes: 'From the beginnings of industrialization, the British working class have enjoyed a reputation for self-education.'[91] Rose recounts 'a broad transformation of the left' beginning with the expanding influence of the Labour Party in the early twentieth century. The gradual shift in the party 'from a working-class self-educated leadership to a middle-class university-educated leadership brought with it a shift from economic protest to cultural protest.'[92] A similar stress is found in the book's unsettling final paragraph, with Rose raising the vital matter that, 'However often today's literary scholars repeat the mantra of race, class, and gender, they clearly have a problem with class.'

Academic journals rightly dedicate reams of pages to gender and race issues, but as Rose points out, the *MLA International Bibliography* produces over a hundred times as many results for 'women' than for 'working class' ('race' produces just over ten times as many), with 'no academic or critical journals anywhere in the world [being] devoted to proletarian literature.'[93] Indeed, the radical (and quite often anarchist) views of Britain's Victorian workers have been neglected by many historians who focus instead on family structure and dietary concerns. Similarly, Richard Gott explains how we know a great deal about 'the generals and proconsuls' of imperial history: 'In recent decades, we have also been told of the contribution to Empire of the "subalterns" and the British working class. Much less familiar are the stories and the biographies of those who resisted, rebelled, and struggled against the Empire's great military machine.'[94]

Rose concludes: 'Affluent and ambitious, profit-motivated and style-conscious, [professionals in the creative industries] are sincerely committed to women's equality and genuinely interested in the literature, music, art, and cuisines of non-Western peoples. But the boutique economy they have constructed involves a process of class formation, where the accoutrements of the avant-garde are used to distance and distinguish cultural workers from more traditional manual workers.'[95] Long gone are the days when Labour politicians concurred with William Paul, member of the syndicalist Socialist Labour Party, who in 1917 advocated for industry to be 'democratically owned and controlled by the workers electing directly from their own ranks industrial administrative committees,' replacing 'the capitalist political or geographical State.'[96]

The lives and writings of pre-war manual workers ('who, it turns out, had a great deal to say') should also give us pause, especially when contrasted with the dazzling bestsellers and 'auto'biographies of countless celebrities which flood the beaches of summer holiday destinations, their vibrant front covers richly decorated with generous *Observer* reviews. With no reality TV shows to debate and no lines from 'satirical' panel shows to quote, many workers spent their time establishing 'mutual improvement' societies, joining libraries and reading contemporary literature, with the reading list of a typical Glaswegian factory worker in the early 1800s putting most undergraduates to shame. Rather than simply being a source of entertainment and pleasure, novels symbolised radicalism and revolution to Victorian factory workers, 'not just because they preached the right kind of left politics, but because they allowed working people to control their own minds.'[97] The late Chartist movement recognized the importance of literature in radicalizing the working classes. Julian Harney wrote in the *Red Republican* that the workers needed the 'Charter and something more.'[98]

In the Jewish East End of London, 'the liberating power of literature was most effectively mobilized by the anarchists and their intellectual leader, Rudolf Rocker.' All ideologies, wrote Rocker, 'were subordinate to the great idea of educating people to be free and to think and work freely.' Rose makes these concerns especially vivid, arguing that many intellectuals feel 'threatened by the prospect of a more equal distribution of culture,' since 'in a society where every man supplies his own philosophy, the philosopher becomes redundant.'[99]

Reversing the Marxist claim that culture is economically determined, and instead arguing that economic systems are culturally determined, Rocker believed, as Rose puts it, that 'the injustices of capitalism would be abolished not by scrapping the Western cultural heritage, but by redistributing it to the workers.'[100] The anarchist claimed with his usual perceptiveness that 'What the human spirit has created in science, art and literature, in every branch of philosophic thought and aesthetic feeling is and must remain the common cultural possession of our own and of all the coming generations. This is the starting-point, this is the bridge to all further social development.'[101] And in spite of this book's literary focus, much work is still to be done in uncovering the anarchist 'seeds beneath the snow' in much of history's great works of art. Susan Watkins is in an important minority in stressing that, 'Historically, the culture of the left, from Marx to Trotsky, Lukács to Sartre, focused overwhelmingly on literature, with far less to say about the visual arts, let along painting.'[102]

The British working classes have also been encouraged to read certain works of literature in order for the gentry to achieve more reactionary goals: 'Disraeli's *Tancred* and George Eliot's *Daniel Deronda*, which both envisioned a Jewish return to Palestine, prepared elite opinion for the Balfour Declaration. Among the masses, the same role was performed by the Sunday schools and church-related day schools, which, while they neglected modern geography, meticulously taught the landscape of the Holy Land.'[103] At the same time, late Victorian farm labourers also found a radicalism in the Bible, as Mabel Ashby explained in her book on her father, *Joseph Ashby of Tysoe*: 'They were on the side of the Prophets, rather than of the Kings, the institutions. The grounds of self-respect their fathers had lost in England they found afresh in Palestine.'[104]

Paul Rayment, the morose protagonist of J. M. Coetzee's novel *Slow Man*, 'tends to trust pictures more than he trusts words,' with the 'immutable' aspects of photography being more than a swift departure from the nature of stories, 'which seem to change shape all the time.'[105] Narratives such as the Genesis myth or *Samson Agonistes* have found themselves in similar positions, their ambiguity resulting in wonderfully broad debates and fresh interpretations, usually socialist or anarchist in character, amongst some of the most impoverished districts in Britain.

Covering a vast range of authors with considerable care, Rose observes, for instance, that 'Though it is usually read as a critique of the class system, *Howards End* is fragrant with nostalgia for a rigid social hierarchy.'[106] And while many radical papers often instinctively denounced Walter Scott's traditionalism, in 1832 'a writer in the Edinburgh *Schoolmaster* ventured that Scott could be read as an anti-Tory, whose lower-class characters were more attractive than his aristocrats.'[107] So too for Daniel Defoe, who collapsed 'all social distinctions into one person': 'In a hierarchical and conformist society that offered little freedom for the laboring classes, *Crusoe* was read as a fable of individualism. It showed what one workingman could do without landlords, clergymen, or capitalists.'[108] Although this struggle to place Britain's schools, universities and workplaces under democratic control has proven to be a difficult one, reminding ourselves of the central issue of education is easy enough, and was perhaps articulated best by Picasso: 'Every child is an artist. The problem is how to remain an artist once we grow up.'[109]

5

Nothing to Declare?

The most important graphic novelist of the twentieth century, Alan Moore, an anarchist and supporter of the Occupy movement, has often structured his work around principles of anti-authoritarianism, collectivism, and a steadfast concern for social justice. His character Promethea is another remarkable and strongly anarchist figure, reflecting Moore's Romantic and Blakean strand of anarchism. Existing as the feminised Titan who, defying authoritarian and religious hierarchies, brought the fire of the gods to man, Promethea explains in her eponymously named comic book:

> There are some people with a vested interest in keeping the world as it is, because that's the world they have power over. You see, in the Immateria [a dimension ruled by imagination], there's no rent, no tax, no property ... no limits.[1]

Promethea seeks to transport people 'From matter ... to mind,' since 'many people only notice the solid world they have been conditioned to think of as more real ... while all about them diamond glaciers creak and star-volcanoes thunder.' She calls this transition 'the end of the world': '"The world" isn't the planet, or the life and people on it. The world is our systems, our politics, our economies ... our ideas of the world! It's our flags and our banknotes and our border wars. I was at Ypres. I was at the Somme. I say end this filthy mess now.'[2]

Like many of Moore's protagonists, Alan Grant's character, the boy genius 'Anarky,' seeks to construct a world devoid of concentrations of private power. Unlike Superman and Batman, 'Anarky feels that he has seen through the great lie that underpins all earthly civilizations ... that Man is a warlike, aggressive creature.'[3] He believes 'The secret of the universe' is 'The common man is always right.' He is convinced, as Shakespeare was, that 'The voice of the people is the voice of God.'[4] In one of the early *Anarky* stories, the twelve-year-old anarchist rallies the homeless to rebel against the building of a new bank on top of their old squatting site. Sensing injustice wherever he goes, Batman subdues him to defend his fellow billionaires. Promoting 'rational analysis' to combat this state-corporate power, Anarky demolishes the illusion of choice in what Niall Ferguson, with his impeccable choice of misleading words, has praised as 'Western democracy': 'Say you don't like your taxes being used to subsidize foreign arms sales for slaughter in the third world. How can you stop it? Vote for somebody else, whose policy is the same? Don't vote?'[5] As Shevek would be quick to point out, citizens of 'Western democracies' may be relatively free in their privileged positions, but 'What they were free to do, however, was another question. It appeared that their freedom from obligation was in exact proportion to their lack of freedom of initiative.'[6]

Not tolerating the handing of social and political direction to a small group of wealthy individuals, Edward Carpenter's sanguine poems in *Toward Democracy* have also been recognised as a paean to the cooperative communities of England:

I see a great land poised as in a dream – waiting for the word by which it may live again.
I see the stretched sleeping figure – waiting for the kiss and the re-awakening.
I hear the bells pealing, and the crash of hammers, and see beautiful parks spread – as in [a] toy show.
I see a great land waiting for its own people to come and take possession of it.[7]

Carpenter, like his friend Morris, didn't openly label himself an anarchist, but his approval of a future 'non-governmental society' and support for syndicalism tie him closely to it. Oscar Wilde, on the other hand, propelled by his commitment to aesthetic and sexual freedoms, told an interviewer in 1894: 'I think I am rather more than a Socialist ... I am something of an Anarchist, I believe; but, of course, the dynamite policy is very absurd indeed.'[8] Although, unlike his genius, he shied away from announcing his anarchist sympathies pubically in fear of the common misconceptions – an assessment of Wilde which his friend Thomas Bell would later confirm.[9] Kropotkin consequently saw Wilde's outstanding essay 'The Soul of Man Under Socialism' as 'that article that O. Wilde wrote on Anarchism.'[10] His outline of anarchism was perhaps an attempt to fulfill a more Bakunin-esque urge for destruction, which he once sardonically explained in a discussion of the Bible: 'When I think of all the harm that book has done, I despair of ever writing anything equal to it.'[11] Along with that of Morris, '[Carpenter and Wilde's] libertarian vision ... remains one of the most inspiring and far-sighted,' for Peter Marshall.[12]

Though not as serious or meticulous, Wilde's florid writings shared the same anarchist outlook as Kropotkin's.[13] Marshall's unsurpassed history of anarchism even goes so far as to claim that Wilde's 'libertarian socialism is the most attractive of all the varieties of anarchism and socialism.'[14] Owen Dudley Edwards goes even further and describes 'The Soul of Man Under Socialism' as 'perhaps the most memorable and certainly the most aesthetic statement of anarchist theory in the English language.'[15] The essay indirectly affirms David Hume's belief that 'Upon these three opinions, therefore, of public *interest*, of *right to power*, and of *right to property*, are all governments founded, and all authority of the few over the many.'[16] It is no surprise, then, that Orwell informed the anarchist George Woodcock that he had 'always been very pro-Wilde.'[17] Thomas

Bell also n[oted] Proudhon's stylistic influences after a long conversation [w]ith Wilde in the summer of 1900.[18] But I am inclined to [dete]ct a closer connection between the Frenchman's critique of [priv]ate property as 'theft!' and the Englishman's idiosyncratic [vi]ew of it as 'a nuisance' in 'Soul of Man.'[19] The rhetoric may [dif]fer, but the underlying assumptions appear to be twinned in i[ntric]ate and subtle ways. Bell qualifies, for instance, that 'in his m[atu]rity [Wilde] was undoubtedly an Anarchist ... philosophic a[nd] humanitarian but clean-cut and plain-spoken, though avoidi[ng] the use of the term Anarchism itself as one likely to cause misu[nd]erstanding in the minds of his readers.'[20]

In his po[lit]ical writings, Wilde adds that 'Socialism, Communism, [or] whatever one chooses to call it, by converting private prope[r]ty into public wealth, and substituting co-operation for [c]ompetition, will restore society to its proper condition of [a] thoroughly healthy organism, and insure the material well-b[e]ing of each member of the community. It will, in fact, give Life [it]s proper basis and its proper environment.' The Irish wit ques[ti]oned the assumption that owning property is a kind of freedo[m], a liberating force which allows an individual to set themselves upon their true desires:

> The posses[s]ion of private property is very often extremely [d]emoralisi[n]g, and that is, of course, one of the reasons why Socialism w[a]nts to get rid of the institution. In fact, property is really a [n]uisance. Some years ago people went about the country sa[y]ing that property has duties. They said it so often and so ted[i]ously that, at last, the Church has begun to say it. One hears it now from every pulpit. It is perfectly true. Property n[o]t merely has duties, but has so many duties that its possession to any large extent is a bore.[21]

Th[e]se anarchist tendencies in Wilde have unfortunately been ov[er]looked by mainstream critics (the reasons for this may be several, as suggested earlier). *The Cambridge Companion to Oscar Wilde* includes not a single indexed reference to 'anarchism' or, astonishingly, 'socialism.'[22] Wilde's notion of 'individualism' in 'Soul of Man' has been interpreted as paradoxical considering his simultaneous urge for socialism, but this seems to me simply Wilde's idiosyncratic term for free expression, self-sufficiency and autonomy ('individualist socialism' should consequently be interpreted as 'libertarian socialism'). His views on other aspects of life are also typically anarchistic. For instance, he took disobedience to be 'man's original virtue':

It is through disobedience that progress has been made, through disobedience and through rebellion ... [M]an thought that the important thing was to have, and did not know that the important thing is to be. The true perfection of man lies, not in what man has, but in what man is ... With the abolition of private property, then, we shall have true, beautiful, healthy Individualism. Nobody will waste his life in accumulating things, and the symbols for things. One will live. To live is the rarest thing in the world. Most people exist, that is all.[23]

This stress on terminological precision has been a prime concern for anarchists. Anarky's 'rational anarchist,' then, should not only question the legitimacy of institutions and governments, but also the self-sustaining authority of terms like 'capitalism' and 'terrorism' as vigorously as the philosopher examines the terms 'object' and 'physical.' The importance of this level of linguistic awareness becomes even more vivid when we realize the fundamentally unjust and self-righteous uses labels like 'anarchism' and 'democracy' can have in all political spaces, from parliament to local activist meetings. An anonymous entry on a popular anarchism library entitled 'What it is to be a girl in an anarchist boys club' reads:

You are approached to answer questions for our group, make decisions and announcements. You even think it is okay to define our group to visitors, strangers. Somehow you aren't ever questioned by the group for this behavior ... Maybe a 'group' discussion dominated by two or three people ISN'T ... It's like you think that calling yourself an anarchist makes you clean and pure and no longer subject to self examination or criticism. You've make the term repulsive to me.[24]

It is with this background that we can interpret Lord Illingworth's remark in *A Woman of No Importance* as being more than simply satirical: 'You can't make people good by Act of Parliament.'[25] Throughout his literary career, Wilde converted his anarchist convictions into elaborate and teasingly imprecise allegories and witticisms. His naturally inventive and irreverent style flourished in novelistic and dramatic form whilst retaining the sense of moral conviction his essays are steeped in.[26] Proceeding with this interpretation, we can easily sympathise with the numerous, early critics (whose views have been picked up by only a handful of their successors) who identified Wilde's short story 'The Young King' as having 'Socialist' leanings, with, for instance, the eponymous self-indulgent protagonist being told by his workers towards the narrative's climax: 'We tread out the grapes, and another drinks the wine. We sow the corn, and our own board is empty. We have chains, though no eye beholds them.'[27] In his society comedies, too, Wilde rebelled against the rigid mores of Victorian England, arguing for a more libertarian and artistic world, since 'Authority is as destructive to those who exercise it as it is to those on whom it is exercised.'[28] Like the anarchists of the Paris Commune and the inhabitants of Huxley's island Pala, Wilde also saw the removal of prisons as a necessary step towards a free world:

The vilest deeds like prison weeds
Bloom well in prison-air:
It is only what is good in Man
That wastes and withers there.[29]

Rejecting such institutional control and domination, he believed with anarchistic zeal that 'authority and compulsion are out of the question. All association must be quite voluntary.'[30] He favoured voluntary association principally because 'people are good when they are let alone.'[31] Wilde would likely have approved of a certain African tribe whose actions have become known through various social media sites and made famous by Dharma Comics. When a member of the tribe does something hurtful to others, they are placed in the centre of the village, and for two days the villagers tell that person every good thing they have ever done. The tribe doesn't see immoral behaviour as stemming from some kind of 'original sin' or evil instinct, to be punished and shamed, but rather it sees misdeeds as cries for help.

One of the most sustained criticisms of anarchism concerns the existence of work and its approach to the nature of the work-shy. It is asked, writes Kropotkin, 'Is not the system of wages, paid in proportion to work performed, the only one that enables compulsion to be employed, without hurting the feelings of independence of the worker?' But this objection is similar to the argument used to justify the state and prisons; namely, because there are a minority who do not obey social customs (often because of the conditions created by the state and prisons to begin with), 'we must maintain magistrates, tribunals and prisons, although these institutions become a source of new evils of all kinds.' Or, 'To avoid a possible evil you have recourse to means which in themselves are a greater evil, and become the source of those same abuses that you wish to remedy. For, do not forget that it is wagedom, the impossibility of living otherwise than by selling your labour, which has created the present

Capitalist system, whose vices you begin to recognize.'[32] Many forget Émile Durkheim's suggestion that 'crime' should not be seen solely as an object of punishment, but it should rather be seen as a useful indicator of where those concerned with social justice should direct their attention.

Similar perspectives on crime were adopted during the establishment of the Paris Commune from March to May 1871. As they were to do over a century later when discussing the Occupy movement, *The Times* discerned in the commune 'the dangerous sentiment of Democracy.'[33] Following the brutal destruction of the Commune, the transportation of the Communards from Paris was, the *Nation* assured its wealthy readers, 'for their mental and moral health.'[34] Despite what the press spun, the abolishing of private property in Paris led to little crime. Following the anarchist scholar Alex Butterworth's lucid account in *The World That Never Was*, after the collectivist society was established on March 28th 1871:

Gambling was banned to save the poor from themselves, the Church disestablished, and three-year moratorium declared on debt. It was only the beginning of what would become an extensive programme of legislation, yet immediately the virtuous example of the Commune seemed to begin trickling down. As the spring sun shone, observers claiming impartiality recorded that, in the absence of envy and oppression, crime spontaneously ceased. Only cynics whispered that the explanation lay in the abductions of troublesome elements by the Commune police under cover of night, or else suggested sarcastically that the criminals no longer had time to break the law, now that they themselves were in power.[35]

Likewise, before Fidel Castro's army entered Havana to impose order after a general strike had deposed Fulgencio Batista, Robert Lyon, Executive Secretary of the New England Office of the

American Friends Service Committee, reported: 'There are no police anywhere in the country, but the crime rate is lower than it has been in years.'[36] Unlike the violence used to defend the Paris Commune, what the recent wave of 'Black Block' anti-corporate activists has brought to the Occupy movement has sometimes been, as Chris Hedges points out, mindless violence which only serves to encourage the myths of rampant violence surrounding anarchism. This is in many ways reminiscent of Bertrand Russell's assessment of the 1890s:

> The impulse towards destruction and violence which has swept over the world began in the sphere of literature. Ibsen, Strindberg, and Nietzsche were angry men – not primarily angry about this or that, but just angry. And so they each found an outlook on life that justified anger. The young admired their passion, and found in it an outlet for their own feelings of revolt against parental authority. The assertion of freedom seemed sufficiently noble to justify violence; the violence duly ensued, but freedom was lost in the process.[37]

Wilde also wrote a perceptive essay on Chuang Tzu, assessing the ancient philosopher in the following, approving way:

> [T]his curious thinker looked back with a sign of regret to a certain Golden Age when there were no competitive examinations, no wearisome education systems, no missionaries, no penny dinners for the people, no Established Churches, no Humanitarian Societies, no dull lectures about one's duty to one's neighbor, and no tedious sermons about any subject at all. In those ideal days, he tells us, people loved each other without being conscious of charity, or writing to the newspapers about it … In an evil moment the Philanthropist made his appearance, and brought with him the mischievous idea of Government.

Wilde concludes: 'All modes of government are wrong. They are unscientific, because they seek to alter the natural environment of man; they are immoral because, by interfering with the individual, they produce the most aggressive forms of egotism; they are ignorant, because they try to spread education; they are self-destructive, because they engender anarchy.'[38] Though most of his essays are characterized by an irreverent, boldly original and anti-authoritarian streak, Wilde's entire anarchistic outlook was perhaps best summarised in this remarkable passage from 'The Soul of Man':

> Man has sought to live intensely, fully, perfectly. When he can do so without exercising restraint on others, or suffering it ever, and his activities are all pleasurable to him, he will be saner, healthier, more civilised, more himself. Pleasure is Nature's test, her sign of approval. When man is happy, he is in harmony with himself and his environment. The new Individualism, for whose service Socialism, whether it wills it or not, is working, will be perfect harmony. It will be what the Greeks sought for, but could not, except in Thought, realise completely, because they had slaves, and fed them; it will be what the Renaissance sought for, but could not realise completely except in Art, because they had slaves, and starved them. It will be complete, and through it each man will attain to his perfection. The new Individualism is the new Hellenism.[39]

With his concerns directed not towards arbitrary competition, but towards self-fulfillment, Wilde held that education should focus on the student learning, not on the teacher teaching. Other anarchists have held that everyone, especially the young, should be allowed to explore in whichever way is suitable for their interests and concerns, and not be treated like mass-produced memory-banks who, in Wilde's words, 'swallow their classics whole, and never taste them.'[40] Echoing Blake, Alexander Malinkov preached something similar in New York in the 1870s, namely that 'in every man there is a divine element. It is sufficient to appeal to it, to find the God in man, for no coercion to be necessary. God will settle everything in people's souls and everyone will become just and kind.'[41] Kropotkin wrote in his memoirs a passage that eloquently draws on this assumption:

> The masses want to know: they are willing to learn; they *can* learn. There, on the crest of that immense moraine which runs between the lakes, as if giants had heaped it up in a hurry to connect the two shores, there stands a Finnish peasant plunged in contemplation of the beautiful lakes, studded with islands, which lie before him. Not one of these peasants, poor and downtrodden though they may be, will pass this spot without stopping to admire the scene. Or there, on the shore of a lake, stands another peasant, and sings something so beautiful that the best musician would envy him his melody, for its feeling and its meditative power. Both deeply feel, both meditate, both think; they are ready to widen their knowledge, – only give it to them, only give them the means of getting leisure.[42]

What's more, the students who read widely outside their course area, whatever degree they take, will generally be penalised with lower grades compared with the more subordinate (and typically less innovative) students whose time is largely devoted to next week's reading list. In order to go beyond this disciplined and myopic 'word-level reading of reality' (of 'liberal,' 'stability,' 'targeted strikes,' 'humanitarian intervention,' and other buzzwords), it becomes necessary to critically approach 'memories, beliefs, values, meanings, and so forth ... which are actually out in the social world of action' and are not to be found in lecture halls.[43] Schools seem to do the opposite, approaching the world from a purely descriptive level before browsing a selection of acceptable truths to develop an understanding of a specific term or ideology, encouraging selective and limited understanding. *Homo sapiens* was made for greater things than this.

New Labour was particularly devoted to teaching children the great achievements of their country, not troubling them with embarrassing truths which might be of some concern to them. Chris Harman explains the historical universal that, 'In higher education, the historians most in accord with establishment opinions are still the ones who receive honours, while those who challenge such opinions are kept out of key university positions.'[44] For the version of history studied in schools, regurgitating dates, names and perhaps the occasional opinion of a Marxist historian, 'knowledge consists simply in being able to memorise such lists, in the fashion of the "Memory Man" or the *Mastermind* contestant.'[45]

In his *Enquiry Concerning Political Justice*, William Godwin noted that, while it is certainly true that the Romans advanced technologically, they nevertheless 'are to be ranked among the foremost destroyers of the human species.'[46] This was a feeling shared by Chomsky in his essay 'Objectivity and Liberal Scholarship':

Quite generally, what grounds are there for supposing that those whose claim to power is based on knowledge and technique will be more benign in their exercise of power than those whose claim is based on wealth or aristocratic origin? On the contrary, one might expect the new mandarin to be dangerously arrogant, aggressive, and incapable of adjusting to failure, as compared with his predecessor, whose claim to power was not diminished by honesty as to the limitations of his knowledge, lack of work to do, or demonstrable mistakes.[47]

In departments of literature, politics, sociology, and philosophy across the country, much reverence is also directed to what Russell would have called the 'intellectual rubbish' which often results from the 'theoretical' views created by many in the humanities, which presumes to critique the corporate takeover of universities using obscure and exclusionist jargon (of the kind Jonathan Rose denounced in the previous chapter). This is often done in the name of radicalism, leftist politics, and even revolution. But this 'theory'-driven turn in academia can also alienate students away from concerted, collectivist political action and the works of anarchist writers (who are already excluded enough from courses in the humanities and social sciences) into secluded, self-congratulatory mania, as the next chapter explores.

6

Intellectual Nonsense and the Fear of Rationality

We are sometimes alone. In those solitary moments when we attempt to make sense of the world, we may harmlessly come across certain books which strike us as vague and obscure, written by philosophers and critics whose knowledge of politics, literature, and cognition appears extensive, backed up with thrilling and unique terminology and numerous hand-picked quotations from physicists and biologists. But things are not as they seem. We are beyond doubt at the wrong side of the library. Through a combination of word-play and fractured syntax, proponents of literary and political theory have released a madness on the world. On this and similar topics, Bertrand Russell wrote to the American philosopher Robert Egner in June 1955: 'At the time when I wrote my *History of Western Philosophy* the Existentialist movement had not yet acquired such a vogue as it has since obtained. I did not mention it because I think it is completely silly and dependent upon elementary mistakes in syntax.'[1]

It should go without saying that the works of the following authors are not entirely filled with the exploitation of scientific and philosophical concepts (what Gilles Deleuze said about education, for instance, seems sensible enough, if not common sense). But the overwhelming tendency amongst all of them is to produce intentionally and aggressively obscure work largely to intimidate their (mostly privileged and Western) audiences into deeming it insightful, radical, and clever.

But before we observe the wreckage and a selection of anarchist responses, a few general comments can provide an important framework. Anthropologists Mary Douglas and Baron Isherwood observe in *The World of Goods* that the standard techniques of maintaining intellectual superiority are 'to erect barriers against entry, to consolidate control of opportunities, and to use techniques of exclusion.' As certain graduate students of politics and critical theory are aware, the person trying to maintain an illusion of intelligence must work to control the discourse, 'Otherwise, his project to make sense of the universe is jeopardized when rival interpretations gain more currency than his own, and the cues that he uses become useless because others have elaborated a different set and put it into circulation.'[2]

The rhetorical barriers often appear quite sturdy. After all, if what the postmodern and poststructuralist enthusiasts are actually saying (beneath the layers of catchphrases like 'symbolic centre,' 'interpolated,' 'what Baudrillard called,' 'différance,' 'the intersection of language, culture, and ideology,' 'problematized,' 'logocentrism,' 'How, then, are we to proceed?,' 's/Subject,' 'heterogeneous structure,' along with the obligatory poetic French or German phrase) can be understood by the person who cleans their windows, then of what use are their jobs? Indeed, throughout radical European history, academic discourse has been far from the central pivot around which campaigners and activists have structured their critiques of state and private power. For the radical republicans of the Elizabethan period, for instance, literature's role was essential, since 'most discussion of the succession question took place in literary and dramatic texts and not official political discourse.'[3]

The widespread unequivocal trust in postmodernist ramblings may reveal something else: that we are afraid of 'those big words which make us so unhappy,' as Stephen Dedalus called them in James Joyce's *Ulysses*. Perhaps the sweeping generalisations and comprehensive 'theories' of the postmodernists and 'semiologists' allow us to feel more at ease, safe in the knowledge that the Marxist's laws of history have offered us the best explanatory account of human affairs. Of course if by 'theory' we mean 'a well-substantiated explanation of some aspect of the natural world, based on a body of facts that have been repeatedly confirmed through observation and experiment' (as the American Association of the Advancement of Science puts it), then the use of the term in departments of literature and politics is misleading to say the least.[4] A social scientist or literary critic calling what they write a 'theory' is a bit like a chemist calling their lab experiments 'poetry.' Peter Medawar recounts in his essay 'Science and Literature' that 'A writer on structuralism in the *TLS* has recently suggested that thoughts which are confused and tortuous by reason of their profundity are most appropriately expressed in prose that is deliberately unclear. What a preposterously silly idea!'[5] One distinguished Shakespearean scholar recently derided 'the current Post-Modernist climate, with its chic neo-Heraclitean dogmas of flux and indeterminacy, of epistemological undecidability and history as the irrecoverably contingent.'[6] Alan Ryan also puts the matter well:

> It is, for instance, pretty suicidal for embattled minorities to embrace Michel Foucault, let alone Jacques Derrida. The minority view was always that power could be undermined by truth ... Once you read Foucault as saying that truth is simply an effect of power, you've had it ... But American departments of literature, history and sociology contain large numbers of self-described leftists who have confused radical doubts about objectivity with political radicalism, and are in a mess.[7]

A typical defence of such authors is that they occasionally write revealing critiques of imperial or neoliberal power. Considering their position of privilege, it's fair to say that this is what their public and students should at least deserve. But their actual presentation and writing style either renders needless confusion, not least because it's emblematic of them to speak in riddles to deflect instant rebuttal; or, they fabricate an understanding of classic philosophical works before setting their own misinterpretations of texts as a gauge to separate the worthy from the unworthy ('You mean to say you don't see, as Žižek does, Leibniz's monadology as a prescient critique of the atomising effects of social networking sites? Then get out!').

Surely one of the most senseless and ridiculous things to have emerged in the two billion years of organic evolution is the feminist 'philosopher' Luce Irigaray's argument that E=mc2 is a sexist equation because 'it privileges the speed of light' – a patriarchal force, like capital letters – 'over other speeds that are vitally necessary to us.' Her critique of fluid dynamics is also inspired, no doubt, by her revolutionary spirit: fluids have been shamefully neglected by physicists, she argues, since 'masculine physics' privileges rigid, solid things over fluids.

Though their doctoral 'research' may beg to differ, obscurantist writers like Irigaray are in fact kicking feminist movements in the teeth by associating them with the irrational, careerist sub-disciplines of Princeton and Yale's comparative literature departments. To get a sense of what similar contributions by other paid academics are like, any 'postmodern generator' paints a fairly accurate picture.[8] A quick game of faking your way through Hegel will also suffice.[9] Woody Allen's short stories often touch on the related theme of pseudo-intellectualism. *The Whore of Mensa* does this brilliantly, as does *My Philosophy*:

I remember my reaction to a typically luminous observation of Kierkegaard's: 'Such a relation which relates itself to its own self (that is to say, a self) must either have constituted itself or have been constituted by another.' The concept brought tears to my eyes. My word, I thought, how clever! (I'm a man who has trouble writing two meaningful sentences on "My Day at the Zoo.") True, the passage was totally incomprehensible to me, but what of it as long as Kierkegaard was having fun?[10]

Similar uses of parody as a means to expose pretension and obfuscation seem to have presented themselves to the young James Joyce, who was asked by Father George O'Neill at the oral examination for his English BA at University College, Dublin, 'How is poetic justice exemplified in the play of King Lear?' Joyce answered, 'I don't know.' 'Oh, come, Mr. Joyce,' O'Neill prodded, 'you are not fair to yourself. I feel sure you have read the play.' 'Oh yes,' replied Joyce, 'but I don't understand your question. The phrase "poetic justice" is unmeaning jargon so far as I am concerned.'[11] He later told his close friend Francini Bruni in Trieste that 'Ideas, classifications, political terminologies leave me indifferent; they are things one has passed beyond. Intellectual anarchy, materialism, rationalism – as if they could get a spider out of his web!'[12] Joyce typically despised high literary talk, remarking of his contemporaries that 'If you took a characteristic obscure passage of one of these people and asked him what it meant, he couldn't tell you, whereas I can justify every line of my book.'[13] John Cowper Powys, a public defender of *Ulysses* during the famous 1933 trial in the US, appropriately wrote in *A Glastonbury Romance* how 'There are human minds – and they find it easy to hypnotise the shallowly clever – who apply to the primordial mysteries of life and sex certain erudite names, and by this naming, and by this noting of certain sequences, they think things are explained.'[14]

As Richard Ellmann records in his monumental biography of the Irishman, Joyce, unwilling to embrace the church, state, or intelligentsia, 'went through a series of violent changes and emerged from them sombre and aloof, except with the few friends to whom he exhibited his joy, his candour, his bursting youth; even with these he was a little strange, never wholly companionable because each time he laid bare his soul he importuned greater loyalty, until friendship became for them almost an impossible burden of submission.' Joyce's parody poem of Eliot's 'The Waste Land' also reveals with a typically subversive wit his intellectual allegiances. Even at the age of 16, in an essay entitled 'The Study of Languages,' Joyce had detected in the distasteful 'tidier' Matthew Arnold (whose spirit, along with that of the Marxist theorist Raymond Williams, to this day shines with a soft, tender glow through the halls of English Literature departments) a mind of 'little opinion.'

Arnold's brother, Thomas, demonstrated a greater penetration than his brother when he explored in one of his letters what John Goode called, commenting on his writings, 'the ineradicable hostility which the progressive mind must feel towards society':

Take but one step in submission, and all the rest is easy ... satisfy yourself that you may honestly defend an unrighteous cause, and then you may go to the Bar, and become distinguished, and perhaps in the end sway the counsels of the State ... All this is open to you; while if you refuse to tamper in a single point with the integrity of your conscience, isolation awaits you, and unhappy love, and the contempt of men; and amidst the general bustle of movement of the world you will be stricken with a kind of impotence, and your arm will seem to be paralysed, and there will be moments when you will almost doubt whether truth indeed exists, or, at least, whether it is fitted for man. Yet in your loneliness you will be visited by consolations which the world knows not of; and you will feel that, if renunciation has separated you from the men of your own generation, it has united you to the great company of just men throughout all past time; nay, that even now, there is a little band of Renunciants scattered over the world, of whom you are one, whose you are, and who are yours for ever.[15]

In all of his work up to *Finnegans Wake*, wrote Ellmann, Joyce 'sought to reveal the coincidence of the present with the past.'[16] 'War and society were not his theme,' he adds, 'but they found him out and forced him into attitudes towards them.'[17] The themes of history and state violence are major ones for Joyce. Although primarily serving as a myopic bigot rather than a historical figure, the citizen of the 'Cyclops' episode in *Ulysses* – in his blind rage against anything foreign – nevertheless touches on the savage, relentless drive of unfettered capitalism to expand its borders, believing corporate advertisements to be 'Swindling the peasants' while the navy 'bosses the earth.'[18] The 'British hyenas' exploited Ireland's comparative advantage and sold it 'in Rio de Janeiro,' accompanied by the obligatory Cromwellian rhetoric like *'God is love'* – a standard pattern for those wielding the 'sword' and 'cannon.'[19] States and their corporate allies are consequently portrayed as inherently violent and expansionist, with the French freely 'mak[ing] an *Entente Cordiale*' with whichever nation happens to be around, only to break it later.[20] The young Stephen Dedalus's suspicion of his classmate's angelic innocence in *A Portrait of the Artist as a Young Man* is strikingly similar to the cynicism of the central protagonist of *Ulysses*, Leopold Bloom, towards the nationalistic views of the citizen of 'Cyclops,' in which he ultimately detects self-serving rhetoric, despite the anti-imperialist undertone.

Imitating a conversation Joyce once had with his friend Ottacaro Weiss, Bloom later claims that 'the history of the world' is replete with 'Persecution ... perpetuating national hatred.'[21] The machinations of state power are held before Bloom's humane moral compass, which condemns 'Force, hatred, history, all that.' As later episodes of *Ulysses* and the extensive letters of its author reveal, Joyce believed history had not only been structured by countless exploitation but was also dominated by fictional legal entities like states and corporations – 'the very opposite of that that is really life,' for Bloom.[22]

More generally, literature for Joyce was not 'a comforting pastime' but rather offered 'grim realizations that dethrone tyrannical secrets in the heart.'[23] But when it came to political science and the Marxist's 'laws' of history, Joyce was 'uniformly sceptical and ironical about all such things.'[24] *Ulysses* casts similar suspicion on Hegelian conceptions of history, with the older Stephen Dedalus regarding a teleological view of history ('the manifestation of God' being its ultimate goal), along with William Blake's rejection of materialism in favour of 'Eternal Reality,' as mere fables.[25] The deadening effects of formal education strengthen this fable-oriented figuration of history, since for 'the boy's blank face[s]' 'history was a tale like any other too often heard.'[26] Joyce's historical perspective emphasises the dominance of ideological and institutional assimilation, being much more rooted in his own experience than in academic abstractions, with these young boys growing up to become a 'mob of young cubs yelling' at Joseph Chamberlain's visit to Trinity College (a personal experience of Joyce's), soon to become 'magistrates and civil servants.'[27]

Democratic developments are also hindered, for Joyce, by the seeming immortality of capitalism and its institutions. We find discussed in *Ulysses* the nature of 'Houses, lines of houses, streets … Changing hands. This owner, that. Landlord never dies they say.' 'Age after age' have 'Pyramids in sand' and 'round towers' been built on 'bread and onions' by 'Slaves,' with the industrial shift from serfs to wage slaves providing little comfort for human values ('No one is anything' on the labour market).[28] One of Dedalus's friends informs him, echoing Kropotkin, that 'The movements which work revolutions in the world are born out of the dreams and visions in a peasant's heart on the hillside,' since those who have not subordinated themselves to power and privilege instinctively feel 'the earth is not an exploitable ground but the living mother.'[29]

Reflecting Joyce's own linguistic proficiency, the development of Dedalus from a reverential catholic schoolboy into an autonomous, intensely detached intellectual is mediated through a variety of literary styles. In his childhood Joyce had 'believed in [the world of ideas] wholeheartedly,' but in maturity 'the minute life of earth claimed him,' and he wielded his considerable literary and philosophical knowledge as weapons against the tyranny of 'those big words ... which make us so unhappy,' as Dedalus calls them (similar to 'The signs that mock me as I go' in Joyce's poem 'Bahnhofstrasse'), in defence of the lives of working class Dubliners.[30] As the critic Fritz Senn understood, instead of blind submission to authority (textual, religious, political), *Ulysses* adopts and teaches a level of scepticism and 'Bloomian reserve' about itself.[31] With a key Joycean technique being the 'fragmentation of word and image,' for Derek Attridge, the ironic comments of Bloom's friend Lenehan simultaneously raise and dash the reader's expectations: 'Expecting every moment will be his next'; 'And with a great future behind him.'[32] They portentously construct themselves into significance but deliver inconsequentiality. One might even argue with the Joyce scholar Hugh Kenner that Joyce's core philosophy of language is embodied in this technique of humane 'irony, relentless irony' – hence his self-mocking postscript to Ezra Pound in June 1920 that his 'poetical epistle ... should be read in the evening when the lakewater is lapping and very rhythmically.'[33] And in the 'Ithaca' episode of *Ulysses*, on the subject of how Bloom and the Dedalus's first met, we find the following passage:

> Did Bloom accept the invitation to dinner given then by the son and afterwards seconded by the father?
>
> Very gratefully, with grateful appreciation, with sincere appreciative gratitude, in appreciatively grateful sincerity of regret, he declined.[34]

By undermining certain 'big words,' Joyce – like the anarchists Orwell and Chomsky – correspondingly flies by the ideological nets of church and state. But unlike Orwell and Chomsky, Joyce always placed irony and literature before morality and politics.

Orwell would have rather documented and acted than spent time in self-indulgence. Chomsky's priorities are also the opposite of Joyce's (although he shares with him a 'dry and sometimes ironical sometimes sarcastic wit,' as his biographer Robert Barsky puts it), hence his general lack of poetic/literary references and citations.[35] Norman Finkelstein once made a similar observation in an interview with Chris Hedges.[36] Perhaps this is disingenuous, but it seems to me that Joyce was never willing to sacrifice literary merit for a just cause (ever), unlike his contemporary Russell. In his later years, Joyce became close friends with Samuel Beckett, as Ellmann records: 'Beckett was addicted to silences, and so was Joyce; they engaged in conversations which consisted often of silences directed towards each other, both suffused with sadness, Beckett mostly for the world, Joyce mostly for himself.'[37] Wilde, too, was described by his one-time attempted collaborator Thomas Bell as 'too much concerned with aesthetics to concern himself with economics, too full of wit to deal seriously at any length with any social question.'[38] Still, these thoughts hardly detract from the importance and insight of Joyce's comic and political vision in works like *Finnegans Wake* and *Ulysses*, and the radically anti-capitalist prose of Wilde's 'The Soul of Man Under Socialism.'

While the citizen of 'Cyclops' denounces imperialism, the 'Circe' episode ardently rejects consumerism (with its confrontational citations of urban Irish culture and popular British songs), which *Ulysses* more generally identifies with Britishness.[39] One of Bloom's transmogrifications in the episode also deplores this state/corporate-dominated conception of nationhood, preferring a more libertarian, anarchistic world:

I stand for the reform of municipal morals ... General amnesty, weekly carnival with masked licence, bonuses for all, esperanto the universal language with universal brotherhood. No more patriotism of barspongers and dropsical imposters. Free money, free love and a free lay church in a free lay state.[40]

These anti-authoritarian sentiments reflect the fact that Joyce was steeped in anarchist philosophy; an important point all too often ignored by mainstream scholarship. He defended it in 1918 on the grounds that 'the state is concentric; man is eccentric.'[41] It is not surprising, then, that Joyce was happiest most under the lax rule of the Austro-Hungarian empire in Trieste.[42] As his literary career progressed, art for Joyce gradually became a mode to challenge the authority of 'my home, my fatherland [and] my church,' echoing what he wrote in secondary school: 'The garb of royalty or of democracy are but a shadow that a "man" leaves behind him.'[43] These conceptual spectres are in *Ulysses* exposed as convenient tools for imperial power. Inspired by his readings of the anarchist Benjamin Tucker and the philosopher Ernest Renan (for whom 'Jesus, in some respects, was an anarchist, for he had no idea of civil government. That government seems to him purely and simply an abuse. ... Every magistrate appeared to him a natural enemy of the people of God'), Joyce has Bloom discuss the notion of a state, deconstructing the notion of homeland and society into a mere spatial abstraction.[44] His protagonist concludes that 'A nation is the same people living in the same place.'[45] Joyce's version of 'Mr. Dooley' bears a similar anti-statist theme, while one of his most successful essays concludes that nationality is 'a useful fiction' for the powerful.[46] To borrow an insight of Jacques Lacan's which Shakespeare's Richard II would have understood well, 'a madman is not only a beggar who thinks he is a king but also a king who thinks he is a king.'[47]

A standard case for colonialism, characterized primarily by a lack of regard for foreign interests, was put forth during Joyce's childhood in Britain by Cecil Rhodes in the 1890s: 'We must find new land from which we can easily obtain raw materials and at the same time exploit the cheap slave labor that is available from the natives of the colonies. The colonies [will] also provide a dumping ground for the surplus goods produced in our factories.'[48] It was a natural corollary for Russell, from these and other elite standards, that 'The aspirations of the labour movement are, on the whole, opposed by the great majority of the educated classes, who feel a menace, not only or chiefly to their personal comfort, but to the civilized life in which they have their part, which they profoundly believe to be important to the world.'[49] The early works of Aldous Huxley examined the effects of imposing imperialist mindsets on the British. In his first novel, he wrote:

> Systematically, from earliest infancy, its members will be assured that there is no happiness to be found except in work and obedience; they will be made to believe that they are happy, that they are tremendously important beings, and that everything they do is noble and significant.[50]

The timeless struggle between clarity and honesty on the one hand, and obfuscation and pretension on the other, which Joyce both engaged in and depicted in his novels, can often be detected in the classic misgivings between analytic and continental philosophy. Speaking on CBS' *Invitation to Learning* programme in 1941, Russell said the following of Hegel's *Philosophy of History*:

> [It] is a very important book indeed, judged by the effects it has had, and a totally unimportant book judged by any truth it may contain. [It is] important, partly because it presented a pattern in history – a scheme, a system – according to which historical events were supposed to have developed, which of course people like. It is a simple formula and they think "now we understand it all" ... [B]ut nobody is wise enough [to

interpret history deterministically]. It is far too complicated and nobody can work it out; and the person who says he has done so is a charlatan.

The renowned Jewish philosopher and Talmudic commentator Emmanuel Lévinas falls clearly onto Hegel's side. One of his many studies of the phenomenological school of philosophy bears the exciting title *Discovering Existence with Husserl*. Like Hegel's *Phenomenology*, its words would no doubt be welcomed amongst small groups of mid-teens narrating their first experiences with LSD: 'To say one doubts reflection is to suppose that reflection at least gives us this doubt itself. Furthermore, when one says that states of consciousness are modified by reflection, one presupposes that the non-modified states are known, for otherwise one could not even suspect the modification, nor even the possibility of reflection itself.'[51] Lévinas's internationally celebrated study continues in much the same rhetorically inflated vain, having been translated into a number of languages, though not, oddly, Hebrew. But perhaps this is for the best – the Jews have suffered enough.

Rudolf Rocker, a self-professed anarchist-without-adjectives (tolerating the co-existence of different schools of anarchism), also would have sympathised with Russell's intolerance for 'intellectual rubbish.' He wrote in *Nationalism and Culture*:

However fully man may recognise cosmic laws he will never be able to change them, because they are not his work. But every form of his social existence, every social institution which the past has bestowed on him as a legacy from remote ancestors, is the work of men and can be changed by human will and action or made to serve new ends. Only such an understanding is truly revolutionary and animated by the spirit of the coming ages. Whoever believes in the necessary sequence of all historical events sacrifices the future to the past. He explains the phenomena of social life, but he does not change them. In this respect all fatalism is alike, whether of a religious, political or economic nature. Whoever is caught in its snare is robbed thereby of life's most precious possession; the impulse to act according to his own needs. It is especially dangerous when fatalism appears in the gown of science, which nowadays so often replaces the cassock of the theologian; therefore we repeat: The causes which underlie the processes of social life have nothing in common with the laws of physical and mechanical natural events, for they are purely the results of human purpose, which is not explicable by scientific methods.[52]

Though his suspicious gaze was cast primarily on eloquence, Francis Bacon's remarks could easily be seen as a valuable lesson to contemporary cultural, literary, and critical studies: '[M]en began to hunt more after words than matter; and more after ... tropes and figures, than after the weight of matter ... [and] soundness of argument.' Unlike Bacon, postmodernists typically reject the rationalist tradition of the Enlightenment, promote a cognitive and cultural relativism which views science as merely a 'narration' or social construction (Paul 'anything goes' Feyerabend and Thomas Kuhn come to mind), and engage in theoretical speculations disconnected from any empirical test. It is not at all clear that any substance can be taken from these views, as Alan Sokal (he of the eponymous 'affair') and Jean Bricmont's devastating study *Intellectual Impostures* makes clear. Through exposing postmodernist's abuse of scientific concepts to lend their own work an aura of prestige, they follow closely in Bacon's footsteps, as do the words of Michael Albert in a review of the book: 'There is nothing truthful, wise, humane, or strategic about confusing hostility to injustice and oppression, which is leftist, with hostility to science and rationality, which is nonsense.'[53]

Sokal and Bricmont reveal the infectious nonsense in the works of Gilles Deleuze, Jacques Derrida, Félix Guattari, Luce Irigaray, Jacques Lacan, Bruno Latour, Jean-François Lyotard, Michel Serres, Paul Virilio and Julia Kristeva. The savage debunking these authors receive in *Intellectual Impostures* provides the reader with vital intellectual self-defence: If Jean Baudrillard writes that modern warfare takes place in a non-Euclidean space, then I shall know he is a member of the Clown Brigade and will be careful with him. Equal caution should be paid to Derrida's thoughts on 'textual' interpretations of the world, viewing as he did 'the text' as an object of profound, even mystical power, to be regarded with fear and awe, and not simply a product of behaviour (like cave etchings or an artist's canvas).

It is equally 'difficult to see,' write Sokal and Bricmont, observing Lacan's musings, 'how the mathematical notion of compact space can be applied fruitfully to something as ill-defined as the "space of *jouissance*" in psychoanalysis.' Where Irigaray sees too much masculinity in science, Lacan can't get enough of it: Trying, in his words, to 'mathematize' everything in sight, he even likens 'the erectile organ' with the square root of -1. 'Thus the erectile organ comes to symbolize the place in *jouissance* ... as a part lacking in the deserved image: that is why it is equivalent to the $\sqrt{-1}$.'

In addition to her remarks on Einstein's equation, Irigaray makes some other astounding claims. Nietzsche, for all his flaws, certainly never 'perceived his ego as an atomic nucleus threatened with explosion,' not least because of the nucleus' discovery being over a decade after the German philosopher's death (she may as well have argued that Thomas Aquinas, when not viewing his kneecaps as πr^2, had nightmares about his music taste contracting diabetes). Demonstrating a peculiar disrespect towards the universe, she continues her attack on the laws of nature by asking, incredibly, 'But what does the mighty theory of general relativity do for us except establish nuclear power plants and question our bodily inertia?'

Similar 'theorists' also often make peculiar use of Marx's claim that 'capitalistic production begets with the inexorability of a law of Nature is own negation.' How they rejoice in borrowing this and similar phrases in discussing how the ideas of their colleagues, on occasion, bring about their own negation etc. Perhaps epitomised best through the stylish work of Slavoj Žižek, empty paradoxes and meaningless reversals are without doubt the order of the day. The majority of opposition to neoliberalism has tended to 'accept many of the basic propositions of neoliberalism,' writes David Harvey.[54] Critiques from critical and political theory departments are no exception, with writers from within the Lacanian and Marxist tradition, who enjoy wordplay and paradox, focusing on internal contradictions rather than systemic faults. Anyone who has read Žižek will most likely regard his books as a dreary sub-genre of science fiction (amazingly, Google Books classes *The Ticklish Subject* as 'Psychology/Physiological Psychology,' while Verso grants it the dubious title of 'Philosophy/Cultural Studies'), their bizarre and often outlandish interpretations of important philosophical texts and popular culture bearing an uncanny resemblance to the work of someone born and raised in a René Magritte painting. A round of Žižuku will put these surrealist visions to rest.[55] Accompanied by Harold Bloom and Jacques Derrida, the contemporary literary theorist with their 'concepts' of 'hermeneutic heterocosm,' 'The Sublime,' and 'hybridity' together appear to be – as divorce lawyers say of their clients' early relationships – 'reasonably happy.' But when unleashed onto works ranging from *Watchmen* to *On Beauty* to *Critique of the Gotha Programme* they produce such vacuous, obscure and fruitless inquiry as to distort even the simplest interpretations of what could be a refreshing and insightful piece of creative writing and artistry.

Though anarchists have traditionally adopted an outlook of

anti-intellectualism and a technique of Orwellian clarity, an abundance of contemporary anarchist theory, by the likes of Saul Newman (founder, father, and only member of the thrilling branch of 'Lacanian anarchism') and the so-called 'post-anarchists,' is drenched in absurd jargon. Even Uri Gordon's insightful study of anarchism borrows Deleuze and Guattari's bizarre and unhelpful terminology from their discussion of knowledge in describing a model of anarchist organisation as 'a structure based on principles of connection, heterogeneity, multiplicity and non-linearity.'[56]

The values of our brazenly individualistic society can be critiqued quite easily without resort to the inflated jargon of *Living in the End Times* or *The Sublime Object of Ideology*: In an essay for *Truthdig*, Chris Hedges explained how 'The fantasy of celebrity culture is not designed simply to entertain. It is designed to drain us emotionally, confuse us about our identity, make us blame ourselves for our predicament, condition us to chase illusions of fame and happiness, and keep us from fighting back.'[57] He opens his book *Empire of Illusion* by comparing the ideologies and narratives which structure the professional wrestling industry with the mainstream media's coverage of political elections. If he wanted to, he could have given such similarities an obscure 'theoretical' name before adding baseless parallels to cosmology or a footnote of Kant's; but, lacking such temptations, he made a choice frowned upon in departments of comparative literature and cultural studies: he wrote in plain English.

As Hedges develops in his extensive journalism, popular culture, the mass media, and positive psychologists promote a surreal form of cheerful conformity, assuring us that if we close our eyes and wish for what we want, if we concentrate on happiness, we will be, in a sense, main characters, drinking our wine, giving each other generous eye contact, and laughing at our sitcoms; smiling protagonists in a tragic-comic episode of an ongoing series of consumerist fantasies.

But the clear and sensible prose of Hedges does not impress those academics loyal to the doctrines of 'theory,' cognitive relativism being one of the most pernicious. As the self-appointed protector of 'womanhood' Germaine Greer explained in a typically scornful article against trans-women, 'feminist fundamentalists hold that biology is a cultural creation.'[58] Postmodernist urges for the similar cases of moral and aesthetic relativism purposefully dodge the questions surrounding the origins of universal biological principles which structure our 'moral grammar' and sense of beauty (the works of John Mikhail and Semir Zeki is especially useful here). And if, as the philosopher and linguist Wolfram Hinzen argues, a naturalistic account of even the simplest lexical items (*house, water*) is beyond our cognitive reach, then we can quickly put aside hopes of 'mathematizing' political and cultural phenomena.[59]

Especially after the rise of the Leninist intelligentsia, Kropotkin was all too aware of this: 'All those sonorous phrases about mankind making progress, while at the same time the progress-makers stand aloof from those whom they pretend to push onwards, are mere sophisms made up by minds anxious to shake off a fretting contradiction.'[60] Bakunin appears to have agreed with Kropotkin: 'Individuals cannot be grasped by thought, by reflection, or even by human speech, which is capable of expression abstractions only ... Therefore social science itself, the science of the future, will necessarily continue to ignore them.'[61]

The charge of cultural illiteracy and conceitedness, of course, is not reserved strictly for po-mo enthusiasts – it can also be directed towards many scientists. Popular science books by Stephen Hawking, Roger Penrose and Michio Kaku all display similar levels of historical ignorance, their concluding feel-good chapters on the relationship between science and religion being an obvious case in point. Together with the postmodernists, they often fail to address the history and nature of science and philosophy, spouting clichés about the incompatibility of the two. Though philosophy has fractured into various domains, much of it is simply early cognitive science (including the theory of ideas, the seventeenth-century shift from ontology to epistemology, aided by Locke and Newton, and speculations on the nature of perception).

One of the greatest contemporary philosophers, Galen Strawson, opens an essay on metaphysics with the following Russellian statement:

> Philosophy is one of the great sciences of reality. It has the same goal as natural science. Both seek to give true accounts, or the best accounts possible, of how things are in reality ... Philosophy, unlike natural science, usually works at finding good ways of characterizing how things are without engaging in much empirical or a posteriori investigation of the world ... Many striking and unobvious facts about the nature of reality can be established a priori, facts about the structure of self-consciousness, for example, or the possibility of free will, or the nature of intentional action, or the viability of the view that there is a fundamental metaphysical distinction between objects and their properties.[62]

The thoughts of Deleuze and Kristeva suddenly appear less overwhelming. Countering their exploitation of 'folk-scientific' intuitions (regarding, for instance, the nature of 'language' and 'truth') requires not only dismantling the grip of postmodernist dogmas on the humanities. It also needs what John Cowper Powys – whose novels will help draw this book to a close – called an 'insanely intense and incorruptible concentration on the mystery of words.'[63] Though group learning, discussion and popular activism play enormously important roles, thoughtful and individual study should not be brushed aside as a mere feat of intellectualism, since, as Cicero reports Cato as saying, 'never is a man more active than when he does nothing, never is he less alone than when he is by himself.' But as Huxley was all too aware: 'Science is not enough, religion is not enough, art is not enough, politics and economics are not enough, nor is love, nor is duty, nor is action however disinterested, nor, however sublime, is contemplation. Nothing short of everything will really do.'[64]

7

Merlin, Glastonbury, and Shakespearean Anarchism

The world is not thy friend, nor the world's law.
The world affords no law to make thee rich.
Then be not poor, but break it, and take this.
Romeo handing gold to the Apothecary, *Romeo and Juliet*, 5.1.72-75

So distribution should undo excess,
And each man have enough.
Gloucester to Edgar, *King Lear*, 4.1.70-71

Alongside Promethea and Chuang Tzu, another seeker of mankind's Golden Age is the wizard Merlin in John Cowper Powys's magnificent 1951 novel *Porius*. One critic called it 'perhaps our century's most profound treatment of the Matter of Britain.'[1] Like most of Powys's novels, it combines the psychological nuance of Joyce with the epic historical narrative of Tolstoy, complemented by the verbosity and wit of the eighteenth and nineteenth-century novelists. Powys's verbosity, however, is that rare variety which maintains its author's sense of humour and irony without ever appearing pretentious (unlike, say, the writings of Will Self). Inspired by the communitarian Golden Age myths of Hesiod and other Greco-Roman literature, Powys's breathtaking prose and insight into what he would frequently refer to as 'Man' is worth a considerable amount of time and thought, and it is astonishing that so few literature departments expose his work to students. For Lawrence Millman, *Porius* 'calls to mind novels as diverse as *One Hundred Years of Solitude*, *Finnegans Wake*, and *Alice in Wonderland*.'[2] If Harry Pollitt had condemned his contemporaries for being 'ashamed of painting the vision splendid,' then Powys's work should be seen as a proud and perseverant answer to this lack of awe at the mysteries of the mind and the natural world.

Porius, Powys's masterpiece, is surely one of the most criminally neglected in the history of literature. It is set in the year 499 during a Saxon incursion towards a Roman fort in North Wales, with King Arthur sending a contingent led by Merlin (or Myrddin Wyllt, as he is predominantly called, possibly a resurrected Cronos as the novel later suggests) to help King Einion and his son Porius defend themselves against the dominant matriarchate. Once he establishes a camp to prepare for the Roman hordes, Myrddin begins to help his companion, the young Neb, persuade himself of the importance of anarchism. After asking him whether obedience is 'a good thing,' the boy replies, shaking his 'impish' head, 'It's what cruel people to do children and animals.'[3] Like Shevek's rejection of 'propertarianism,' Myrddin sees beyond the cynical Christian definition of 'love' and the tendencies towards domination and ownership this doctrine evokes: 'I tell you wherever there is what they call "love" there is hatred too and lust for obedience! What the world wants is more common-sense, more kindness, more indulgence, more leaving people alone.'[4]

These ideas have partly been supported by Michael Sandel in his critique of Rawlsian liberalism. Sandel argues that notions of justice can only emerge in the absence of feelings like fraternity and benevolence.[5] Though no anarchist I am aware of would go this far, it is worth considering the impact and, one might argue, clouding effects over-indulging in social interaction can have in the consideration of social justice. Hume, for instance, remarked that the 'nobler virtues' of fraternity and benevolence, if increased, would sideline justice to a less central position of importance in social revolution. Perhaps closer to Powys's anarchism is Kropotkin's philosophy, which Myrddin would have appreciated:

It is not love and not even sympathy upon which society is based in mankind; it is the conscience – be it only at the stage of an instinct of human solidarity. It is the unconscious recognition of the force that is borrowed by each man from the practice of mutual aid; of the close dependency of everyone's happiness of all; and of the sense of justice, or equity, which brings the individual to consider the rights of every other individual as equal to his own. Upon this broad and necessary foundation the still higher moral feelings are developed.[6]

The primacy of justice and morality in human political instincts is a major theme in *Porius*. Having repressed any attempts by potential leaders to direct and command society, the forest people of Powys's Wales are the most anarchistic of its various tribes. Their 'whole way of life was non-Aryan and non-Celtic. It was communistic and matriarchal, tempered by the druidic magic that had reached them from the survivors of the last continent of Atlantis' (the lost underwater city is mentioned in a few of Powys's novels, largely because it represented for him, as it does for Dave Spear in *A Glastonbury Romance*, an anarchist society).[7] But unlike the wizard, the forest people are far from utopic, as Porius's father, Prince Einion, explains: 'The forest people have *never had* a "Golden Age," and never will. They're beyond it ... [A]nd that's why we can't – why nobody ever will – really conquer them.'"[8] They may well have read Hedges, who argues in *I Don't Believe in Atheists* that any utopic philosophy, whether socialist or Objectivist, inevitably ignores at its peril the moral and cognitive 'scope and limits' (Russell) of humans.

These anti-patriarchal instincts are also found in the novel's protagonist, whose wish to obey women stems from an anarchistic urge to ally himself against the illegitimate and oppressive authority of the patriarchal Christian church and the Roman Empire. When in the company of women, he often 'experienced an automatic desire to be guided by a smile, a nod, a shake of the head.'[9] In Porius's anarchistic mind, even the plants and rivers continually rebel against external authority, leading him to tell his closest friend, Rhun, 'I like this time of twilight down here by the river ... the river seems more conscious of your existence than the woods and precipices.'[10] Sharing much of Porius's approach to the natural world, one particularly striking passage in David Foster Wallace's novel *Infinite Jest* relatedly suggests that the world's objects should be treated and handled as if they were our own body – much like, Wallace candidly suggests, the economical movements and 'animal grace' of Marlon Brando.[11]

With metaphors of instinctive liberation and animacy (mediated through Powys's vivid depictions of the natural landscape) still fresh in the reader's mind, Bakunin's 'instinct fo freedom' finds new meaning in the following Tolkien-esqr passage:

Porius felt it was infinitely preferable for the unnumbred gods and men and spirits and elements and beasts and lrds and fishes and reptiles and worms and insects an all vegetation and for the air and the earth and the sun ad the stars and all the waters to have nothing to struggl with beyond themselves, and nothing to compete with beyond themselves, and nothing to punish them or rewad them beyond themselves, save only that mystery of mysteies, that liberator of liberators, that everlasting friend of he Many against the One, Tyche Soteer, "Chance, the Saviou."[12]

More generally, Powys's philosophical musings appear to be similar to those of Kant, Ivan Karamazov (he praisedDostoevsky as the greatest of all novelists, admiring the 'mood of ecstasy ... in which Alyosha Karamazov kissed the earth witl sobs'), and, by his own reckoning, Shakespeare.[13] Lecturing at Columbia University in 1930, he claimed with his usual verve that

Shakespeare – who, through the mouth of Timon of Athens, saw gold as the source of all evil – was 'naturally an anarchist':

> King Lear was a spoilt child: he later became an anarchist. The moral attitude of civilization and society is attacked in Lear. Jacques in *As You Like It* is an anarchist. Caliban was not only an anarchist against the ways of man: he represents the revolt of *the Cosmos against the Human Race*.[14]

Powys also sympathised with the 'Communist system of social justice,' but not with 'the Communist philosophy: for I feel that the deepest thing in life is the soul's individual struggle to reach an exultant peace in relation to more cosmic forces than *any* social system, just or unjust, can cope with or compass.'[15] In *A Glastonbury Romance*, the views of the anarchist Paul Trent seem closest to those of his creator than any other character in the novel. He tells one of the grand and rather discourteous old ladies of Glastonbury, Elizabeth Crow, about the communist Dave Spear, a friend and fellow revolutionary:

> 'What I've found is,' he went on eagerly, quite oblivious of this snub, 'that none of these people, that you quite properly call politicians, Miss Crow, know what liberty is. The capitalists take liberty away from us in the name of liberty, which, under them, means liberty to work like a slave, or, to starve. But your relative Mr. Spear isn't much better! He takes liberty away from the individual in the name of the community. So there you are, you see! I am probably the only *man* in Glastonbury who fights for real liberty – which means, of course, a voluntary association of free spirits to enjoy the ideal life.'[16]

While the anarchists have always held that humans are strictly part of nature ('Man is part of Nature,' explained Russell, 'not something contrasted with Nature'), communism has typically viewed man as a half-finished product who tries to overcome the natural world he finds himself in.[17] Hedges consequently writes that 'As long as the Earth is viewed as the personal property of the human race, a belief embraced by everyone from born-again Christians to Marxists to free-market economists, we are destined soon to inhabit a biological wasteland.'[18] Communism also entails the private ownership of production, and so does not create the conditions under which manual and intellectual labour can both come under an individual's direction and also provide a fulfilling, creative outlet. Marshall S. Shatz adds: 'To the anarchists, Marxism has always represented not just a misguided and potentially dangerous set of tactics for achieving the downfall of an order they both ostensibly rejected, but a fundamentally different perception of the world and of man's purpose in it.'[19] Powys explains his belief in a key distinction between communism and anarchism in the following passage from his autobiography

I have often wondered how I would get on in Soviet Russia to which I feel as much attracted as I do to the Catholic Church. I am so simple in my tastes, and so unambitious, that as long as I had the smallest room to myself and enough kopecks to keep me in bread and tea and cigarettes, and as long as I had a road, or even a path across a common, where I could walk alone, I believe I could be happy there. Only I should be always wanting to share the contents of my samovar with some mystical Father Zosima. I fully agree that I ought to be forced by a Communist State to share the burden of manual labour. But, when I've done my share, I want to be free *to turn from the State altogether*, and from all my tedious mundane concern, free to discuss God and Freedom and Immortality with learned and pious men! Yes, I agree altogether with my Communistic friends that I ought to be forced to do some sort of manual labour. But I do not agree with them that it is a waste of time to discuss God. It is not that I myself ever want to go to church. I never feel the remotest desire to do so; and when I pray, as I weary myself with doing, I pray to idols and fetishes and images, to sticks and stones, to the Sun and the Moon and the Earth.[20]

The Marxist philosophy of education has typically held that education should above all bring class consciousness to workers. Judith Suissa's compelling study *Anarchism and Education* summarises that, 'While anarchists share with Marxists many assumptions regarding the nature of labour in capitalist society, the anarchist perspective on social change and the role of the state leads to a very different conception of vocational education.'[21]

Both the anarchists and Marxists, then, while agreeing on many things, have quite different conceptions of the relationship between human nature and nature itself. With Marxism,

nature is something that man must master; he asserts himself over it, and harnesses it to his own purposes. There is an inherent opposition between man and nature that is expressed in man's quest to gain control over the forces of nature through his labor, to turn them to productive economic purposes, and to create the man-made world in which his own nature will realize itself.[22]

Hence we find Trotsky's disdain for the blind and mechanical natural world in his 1930 study *The Russian Revolution*: 'The historic ascent of humanity, taken as a whole, may be summarized as a succession of victories of consciousness over blind forces – in nature, in society, in man himself.'[23] The anarchist, as we have seen, deals with quite different forces and concerns. Through anarchism, unlike Marx's authoritarianism, humanity's relationship with nature is seen to be one of harmony: 'Human society is not a collective enterprise for the mastery of nature but an organic outgrowth of nature, and the ills of society stem from efforts to impose artificial constraints on its free, spontaneous development.'[24] To the anarchist (and we might say to the musician, the artist, and a whole host of other thinkers, scientists and explorers), life is primarily directed by the urges of imagination and inquiry. The natural world cannot be continually moulded. The communist, with his closed environment, does not harbour and encourage this spontaneous development. On this and much else, Powys sided firmly with the anarchists:

> In action we may be weak and clumsy blunderers, or on the hand sometimes incompetent and sometimes competent. All this is largely beyond our control. What is *not* beyond our control is our *feeling* about it.
> 'I am a cowardly, blundering, incompetent worm.'
> Very good. So be it. But it is in my power to be a worm with a deep, calm, resolute cheerfulness, if not with a magical exultation.[25]

John Crow, a central character in *A Glastonbury Romance*, at one point lies with his lover Mary and thinks to himself: 'Don't let me ever compete with anyone! ... If I'm a worm and no man, let me enjoy my life as a worm. Let me stop showing off to anyone; even to Mary! Let me live my own life free from the opinions, good or bad, of all other people! Now that I've found Mary, let me want nothing else!'[26] On his way to Glastonbury, being driven across the hills of Somerset, John later looks upon the rural scenery and sees in it an anarchistic urge for self-fulfillment:

> The wide Plain stretched around them, cold and mute, and it was as if the daylight had ceased to perish out of the sky, even while the surface of the earth grew dark. The identity of that great space of downland was indrawn upon itself, neither

listening nor seeking articulation, lost in an interior world so much vaster and so much more important than the encounters of man with man, whether evoked by prayer or by chance, that such meetings were like the meetings of ants and beetles upon the twilit terrace that had thoughts and memories of its own altogether outside such infinitesimal lives.[27]

'No ruling authorities, then,' Kropotkin concludes from a similar appreciation of human autonomy. 'No government of man by man; no crystallization and immobility, but a continual evolution such as we see in Nature.'[28] Anarchism 'wishes to release the natural forces of the personality rather than control them the better to direct them into economically productive areas'; and not have it suppressed or moulded by the dominant economic institutions, ecclesiastical forces, and the values and concerns of the media.[29] According to Herbert Read, the anarchist, unlike the existentialist, 'just doesn't feel that *Angst*, the dreadful shipwreck on the confines of the universe, from which the existentialist reacts with despairful energy. He agrees with the marxist that it is merely a modern myth. He draws in his metaphysical horns and explores the world of nature [sic].'[30] Anarchism, concludes Read, 'is the *only* political theory that combined an essentially revolutionary and contingent attitude with a philosophy of freedom.'[31]

According to his autobiography, the life of Powys, like that of Russell's as he also records in the preface to his autobiography, was directed for him by a series of 'rather discordant elements': 'a desire to enjoy the Cosmos, a desire to appease my Conscience, a desire to play the part of a Magician, a desire to play the part of a Helper, and finally a desire to satisfy my Viciousness.'[32] He largely avoided the company of other literary figures, keeping to himself and becoming over time what Philip Larkin would describe as a 'gigantic mythopoetic literary volcano.'[33] Out of the intense loneliness of his younger years emerged a mature, original writer of literary masterworks, the best of which, in their romantic and philosophical scope, match any of Dostoevsky's:

> How often in my life there have come such moments when I have turned away in sullen apathy from the tribal activity into which I have been flung! I can recall the feelings so well with which at such times I have hunted round in my recalcitrant mind for a fellow-Ishmael, or Ishmaeless, and found none. I can remember once ever so much later – when we lived at Montacute – feeling aggrieved with every member of our large family – and walking along up the lane, beyond Mr. Marsh's farm, in the direction of Thorn Cross, searching for this unknown fellow outcast.[34]

With Shevek breaking down psychological and ideological walls, Powys agrees to lend his own energies to the struggle, writing in *A Glastonbury Romance* that 'It's the policeman in our minds ... that stops us all from being ourselves and letting other people be themselves.'[35] One of his later novels, *Atlantis*, concerning Odysseus, echoes these anti-authoritarian concerns: Having returned home to Ithaca, the man of the 'nimble wits' embarks on a voyage to Atlantis, recently submerged during an uprising of the Titans – breaking free from Tartarus – against the Olympian gods. As Kratos of *God of War* fame would appreciate, this leads to a 'multiversal revolt against the authority of the Olympians' and 'as a result of a spontaneous and natural revolt all over the world against god-worship, all the gods that exist, from Zeus downwards, and all the goddesses that exist from Hera downwards ... are fated to perish ... the fatal sickness that must ere long bring them to their end is caused by this growing refusal to worship them.'[36]

The Titans would doubtless have concurred when Porius's aged Auntie Esyllt urges him as a child to realise that no authority, 'Neither Life nor Death nor Love nor Hate nor Angles nor Devils nor Mind nor Matter nor Present nor Past – No! nor even the Blessed Trinity Itself – has any power to meddle with the *individual human will.*'[37] Powys had earlier justified this to some degree in his autobiography: 'Size, distance, boundlessness never worry me much. I regard them as a mathematical tricks – almost an illusion – not to be compared with the expansiveness of the mystery of thought, thought which grasps them, encloses them, surmounts them.'[38] Through the mediation of subtle tropes and symbolism, the narrative of *Porius* seems to hint that its protagonist's admiration for wind ('the power he worshipped beyond all the other elements') stems from a deep respect for the equally invisible power of free will.[39] It is with a similar antinomianism to Blake's that he also rejects Christianity's binary moral distinctions: 'I don't see things in that light, and never shall.'[40]

Rejecting, with Anarky and Morris (who promoted man's 'innate socialism'), the popular myth of humanity's predominantly selfish proclivities, Porius's mentor Brother John believes passionately that 'The heart of man ... is *naturally good!*' and that only the cruel promote the doctrine politely referred to today in distinguished economics textbooks as 'the profit motive,' summarized here by Gabriel Ardant, admittedly with some exaggeration: '*Homo oeconomicus* has no feeling of affection for his fellow man. He wishes to see in front of him only other economic agents, purchases, vendors, borrowers, creditors, with whom he has in theory a purely economic relationship.'[41] The economic man is supposed to be, like Mr. Lau, good with calculation. This is more elaborately portrayed by Brother John as the claim that 'the simple minds of our ordinary Gaer people ... [contain] deep hell pools and dark Tartaruses of abominations of which they themselves are totally ignorant.'[42] It is factors similar to these which have led the critics Charles Lock and Norman Denny to claim that the novel has wider implications for the medium:

Porius cannot be domesticated ... [I]ts wildness, its challenge to normative ideas of morality and perception, is so great that if we were to embrace it we would have to jettison those attributes of the novel which have enabled it to continue as a living phenomenon and, in the 'right' hands, be both commercially lucrative and socially sanctioned.[43]

Porius's celebration of individual choice over the arbitrary dictates of power also stimulates his remarkable interpretation of the Genesis myth during his childhood. After spying 'a picture of the infant Jesus playing with a snake' in his mother's bedchamber, he comments that the young Christ

was lovingly and obstinately thwarting the one supreme desire of his dangerous plaything, *the desire to escape*. This desire had smouldered into such a recoil of tragic desperation that even as a boy Porius has read in the one small saurian eye which alone was visible the shuddering resolve, *sooner than not to escape*, to drag the world's hope of redemption down with him!

"It wants to escape," Porius said to himself ... "It wants to escape into Nothingness; and if God won't let him, he's ready to drag Creation down with him!"[44]

John Crow shares a related disrespect for artificial creations, with his admiration being directed instead towards the world of mind, not matter: '"Let these things of gilded vapour," he thought, "these things of tinsel and tin have their day! Let the savage opposites of them have their day too. They are all dreams, all dreams within dreams, and the underlying reality beneath them is something completely different from them all."'[45] Like John Geard, the man of the 'planetary consciousness' who, because of the dream-like nature of wakefulness, refers to the notion of the next life as 'the next dream,' Sam Dekker also 'felt as if he were living in two worlds at the same time, and one of them, by far the less real and by far the more absurd, was trying to convince him that the other was a fantasy' (to which the philosopher Donald Davidson would have replied, as he used to wryly put it, we live in one world 'at most').[46] Here is Porius again: 'I've no music in me, no poetry in me, no love in me. And yet I had an ecstasy just then. I *can* have an ecstasy as well as another, though I *have* no music, no poetry, no love, and enjoy nothing in life but life and trying to analyze it!'[47] The protagonist's physical movements are described at one point as being 'accompanied by the rapid movements of thoughts so detached, so uninvolved, so independent, that it was a wonder they didn't paralyze the natural reactions of his senses or reduce them to a tantalized sullenness.'[48]

Crow's wife, Mary, often rejects her husband's philosophical musings, with Powys believing that 'Perhaps a girl's nerves respond to the nerves of another girl and send out magnetic currents that can be caught from far off; whereas something in the masculine constitution, something dense, think, obtuse, *stupid*, has the power of rejecting such contacts. Or it may be that the erotic emotions, when they brim over from the masculine spirit, extricate themselves, as women's feelings never do, from the bitter-sweet honeycomb of Nature, and shoot off, up, out, and away, into dimensions of non-natural existence, where the nerve-rays of women cannot follow.'[49] Crow later watches a herd of sheep moving up a hill in the Somerset countryside, and the figures of a man, a boy, and a sheep-dog walking behind them:

As he watched these figures and that moving river of grey backs in front of them his mind was carried away on a long vista of memories. Various roads where he had encountered such sights, some of them in Norfolk, some of them in France, came drifting through his mind and with these memories came a queer feeling that the whole of his life was but a series of such dream-pictures and that the whole series of these pictures was something from which, if he made a strong enough effort, he could awake, and feel them all dispersing, like wisps of vapour. Pain was real – that woman crying out upon her cancer and calling it 'Lord! Lord!' – but even pain, and all the other horrors of life seemed, as he stared at the backs of those moving sheep, to be made of a 'stuff', as Shakespeare calls it, that could be compelled to yield, to loosen, to melt, to fade, under the right pressure.[50]

Though he is urged instead by impossible riches and not by Crow and Porius's anti-authoritarianism, Shakespeare's Marcus Andronicus pleas likewise:

If I do dream, would all my wealth would wake me.
If I do wake, some planet strike me down
That I may slumber an eternal sleep.[51]

One of the *Porius*'s central concerns is how the protagonist, like Milton's Samson, navigates himself away from an unshakeable urge to rid himself of the troubles of self-awareness by submerging into the sea (composed of that watery element Powys saw much mystery in) 'out of which all life originally sprung.' As John Geard in *A Glastonbury Romance* slowly drowns at the climax of the novel, the narrator speculates on the nature of his death: 'While many pathological subjects, this writer maintains, seek a pre-natal peace in death, what Mr. Geard in his planetary consciousness desired was a return to that remote and primal element of Water, which was literally the great maternal womb of all organic earth-life.'[52] We learn on the next page that, as with the novel's author, 'Mr. Geard's character will never be understood – or the monstrous inhumanity of his departure from the visible world condoned – until it is realised that the unruffled amiability and the unfailing indulgence of his attitude to those near and dear to him concealed a hidden detachment from them that had always been an unbridged gulf.'[53]

As with Moore's Promethea, who sought to bring about the end of 'the world' through deconstructing dangerous ideological frameworks of interpretation, Porius seeks to end it not by violent acts of heroism, but by what J. M. Coetzee's protagonist in *Slow Man*, Paul Rayment, calls 'some purely mental act.'[54] These concerns become particularly vivid when the urge to return to 'Nothingness' is indeed fulfilled, but not for the reasons Porius hoped, with dissidents being frequently murdered by the church 'because they had wiser and kindlier thoughts than those in power and because they spoke what they thought.'[55]

A comparable interpretation of the Genesis myth to Porius's is found when Myrddin, sitting on a raft in the middle of a calm stream, suddenly realises the presence of a rat on his hand licking his knuckles: '"So you, water rat," he thought, "you alone of all my creatures have dared to disobey me! For this disobedience may your children ... have luck ... and safety beyond safety from all their enemies!"'[56] With similar dialogues rejecting Urras's 'Principle of Superiority' from *The Dispossessed*, we soon find that the crux of the novel, and the heart of anarchism itself, is a rejection of arbitrary and oppressive authority. Nowhere is Powys's version of this theme more thoroughly explicated than through Myrddin – that 'protosocialist dreamer,' for Bernard Dick.[57] To return finally to his discussion with Neb, the inquisitive child asks 'What turns a god into a devil, Master?' The wizard replies:

> Power, my son. Nobody in the world, nobody beyond the world, can be trusted with power, unless perhaps it be our mother the earth; but I doubt whether even she can. The Golden Age can never come again till governments and rulers and kings and emperors and priests and druids and gods and devils learn to unmake themselves as I did, and leave men and women to themselves![58]

Myrddin tells the young boy how this Second Golden Age will be brought about 'By putting an end to all tyrants, dictators, despots, rulers, priests, and governments. By putting an end to myself – *as a god* – and leaving men and all the children of earth – alone!'[59] Not least because 'there is probably no modern poet more correct than Shakespeare,' as Schlegel put it, Lord Talbot in *Henry VI, Part I* seems to have had a similar view to Myrddin's:

> But kings and mightiest potentates must die,
> For that's the end of human misery.[60]

Shakespeare, who wrote not a poem or elegy to mark the death of Queen Elizabeth or the ascension of King James, had no sympathy for 'a hierarchic social system of inherited, permanent and inalterable class and rank ... whose verticality was ordered on the pattern on the cosmos itself.'[61] For Shakespeare, argues Victor Kiernan in seminal work, the 'animating spirit' of the state is 'an unreasoning, insatiable thirst for power.'[62] Quite like the socialist plays of Edward Bond (most notably *Lear*), Shakespeare's dramas rejected the submission of the commoner to the will of authority, both regional and national, along with the muffled obedience of women.[63] But unlike the works and political leanings of writers who claim to have learned much from Shakespeare (Ian McEwan, Martin Amis, Julian Barnes, Stephen Fry – who proved himself a judicious scholar of Shakespeare during his Cambridge years by using what he modestly describes in his second autobiography as his 'creepily good' memory to develop a 'theory of Shakespearean tragic and comic forms' to use as a template to answer any conceivable essay question), 'subversive assertion of class and rank as the betrayal of an essential human commonality is widely found in the Histories.'[64] Hence we find in *King Lear* the playwright heroising an anonymous servant for drawing his sword against the Duke of Cornwall for torturing Gloucester, dramatising Renaissance resistance theory.[65]

Commenting on *Henry VI, Part 2*, which depicts the famous uprising of Jack Cade in 1450 against the corrupt gentry, John Palmer remarked in his 1948 study *Political Characters of Shakespeare*, not often read today, that 'It is strange that those who find in Cade's barbarity an indication of Shakespeare's horror of the mob should neglect to find in the barbarity of Queen Margaret or of my lords Clifford and York an indication of his horror of the nobility.'[66] The play observes the manifold injustices of the judicial system, noting that those who benefited from the rare privilege of literacy could escape execution for murder.[67] It depicts the English state as a corrupt, torture-loving, and over-taxing burden on common life, with Richard of Gloucester stating, 'Priests pray for enemies, but princes kill.'[68] Perhaps the most careful and important study of Shakespeare's radicalism in more recent times is the Rutgers scholar Chris Fitter's 2012 book on the playwright's early career. After his first decade of writing, Shakespeare emerged from the turbulent 1590s an 'audacious and committed ... nuanced and powerful protest playwright.'[69] Using a unique mix of deixis (making reference to the context of the particular performance), framing and doubling, Shakespeare's stagecraft served to disrupt the incorporation of spectators into 'a range of state ideologies,' argues Fitter with substantial textual and historical support. But the claim that Shakespeare was a radical remains a minority view amongst 'the almost immeasurable ocean of Shakespeare studies.'[70] Departing from the received wisdom of mainstream scholarship, Fitter sees Shakespeare's drama more as scripts than plays or texts, 'scripts whose dialogues are crafted for placement in *further* dialogue: with a gathered crowd, in a certain locus, within a specific cultural milieu. The insistence that Shakespearean drama essentially comprised not verse narratives but a set of flexible playscripts, aiming at a self-unfolding through action on a stage, not turning the page, is inestimably important.'[71] Shakespeare's plays are easily adaptable for public theatres and improvise venues, encouraging a dynamic and innovative use of these political scripts. Moreover, they appealed not just to the breadwinning artisan and labourer, but to youth culture, women, and other discontents.

Fitter points out that critics (such as the Cambridge School political theorists) have rarely drawn connections between Shakespeare's drama and the radical currents in Tudor and Stuart England. The 1590s (the 'Black Nineties,' for Fitter) saw the Oxford Rising of 1596 and Hackett's Rebellion on 1591, both of which, as *Richard II* and *Henry VI, Part 2* reveal, influenced Shakespeare's politics. When Shakespeare began his career, arriving in London in the late 1580s, he would have been surrounded by stark wealth disparities (depicted in *As You Like It* and through the cries of the malnourished protestors in *Coriolanus*) and various resentful Armada mariners organising to demand payment for their service or basic provisions for their time at sea, which the crown summarily refused them. In 1589, 'When a crowd of 500 discharged soldiers assembled … near the royal palace in Westminster to protest their non-payment Provost-Marshals hauled out four and hanged them, while calling out 2,000 men from the city's trained bands.'[72] Many Londoners consequently felt no more loyalty to England than they did to Spain, with one Canterbury artisan complaining in 1596, 'If the Spaniards did inhabit here it would be better for us … [for] we could not live worse unless we were starved.' Like the Levellers and Ranters soon to come after him, Bartholomew Steere called for popular revolt in 1596 and stated that England 'would never be well untill some of the gentlemen were knockt downe,' not least because 'the common long sithens in Spaine did rise and kill all gentlemen … and sithens that times have lyved merrily there.'[73] Fear of the public and a heightened awareness of their own small numbers were defining features of the gentry in the late sixteenth century. As an Essex labourer had asked two years before Steere, 'What can riche men do against poore men yf poore men rise and hold toguither?'[74]

The post-revisionist school of early modern English political history has revealed that the commoners of Tudor England were far from pre-political and ideologically docile, with the country housing 9,000 parishes run by up to 50,000 men in total.[75] Given all this, Fitter is more than justified in arguing the Shakespeare's focus on state and ecclesiastical figureheads 'demonstrates not antipopulist snobbery (a literary critical indictment frequently imputed) – for the impact of policy, convulsing commoners' lives, is never far away – but reflects rather ... the enforced contemporary gaze of the hyperactive political nation, in late Tudor England's polymorphous state.'[76] Shakespeare's position towards insurrection seems to have been similar to that of the sixteenth-century political philosopher Thomas Starkey, who in his *Dialogue between Pole and Lupset* has the former claim that, since tyranny resulted from the fall of man and was not God's creation, men have the right to usurp tyrants.[77]

Like Shakespeare and a host of subsequent English playwrights, Bakunin and Kropotkin saw the state, as the fine anarchist scholar Lucien van der Walt summarises, as 'a centralised, hierarchical system of territorial power, run by and for the ruling class,' maintained through repression at home and imperialism abroad.[78] In his analysis of the state's historical role, Kropotkin begun by emphasising that trying to abolish the 'state' is not the same as trying to abolish 'society' or any form of organisation; anarchism is rather, as Wayne Price puts it, 'democracy without the state.'[79] Joseph Lane strongly agreed in his *An Anti-Statist Communist Manifesto* of 1887. Herbert Read explained things plainly in *Poetry and Anarchism*:

> Government – that is to say, control of the individual in the interests of the community, is inevitable if two or more men combine for a common purpose; government is the embodiment of that purpose. But government in this sense is far removed from the conception of an autonomous state.[80]

Discussing one his major influences, Dostoevsky's *The Brothers Karamazov*, Powys explores his rejection of authority through the mouth of Dr. Fell in *A Glastonbury Romance*, who tells one of Glastonbury's more anarchistic residents, Tom Barter, on a particularly rainy night:

> I read a Russian book once, Barter, by that man whose name beings with D, and a character there says he believes in God but rejects God's World. Now I feel just the opposite! I think the whole of God's World is infinitely to be pitied – tortured and torturers alike – but I think that God himself, the great Living God, responsible for it all, the powerful Creator who deliberately gave such reptiles, such sharks, such hyænas, such jackals as we are, this accursed gift of Free Will, ought to have *such a Cancer* ... as would keep him Alive and Howling for a Million Years![81]

Sam Dekker later informs his friend Owen Evans of his equally unconventional, Tolstoyan approach to religion, which bears some similarities with Porius's vision of the infant Jesus:

> My Christ's like Lucifer – only he's not evil ... at least not what I call evil. But He's the enemy of God. That is, He's the enemy of Creation! He's always struggling against Life, as we know it ... this curst, cruel self-assertion ... this pricking up of fins, this prodding with horns ... this opening of mouths ... this clutching, this ravishing, this snatching, this *possessing*.[82]

When Powys introduces the eponymous protagonist of his 1929 novel *Wolf Solent*, we find a comparable intolerance for the aloof promises of a brighter future found not only throughout large parts of Christian history, but also in liberal democracies today:

One of the suppressed emotions that had burst forth on that January afternoon had had to do with the appalling misery of so many of his fellow Londoners. He recalled the figure of a man he had seen on the steps outside Waterloo Station. The inert despair upon the face that this figure had turned towards him came between him now and a hillside covered with budding beeches. The face was repeated many times among those great curving masses of emerald-clear foliage. It was an English face; and it was also a Chinese face, a Russian face, an Indian face. It had the variableness of that Protean wine of the priestess Bacbuc. It was just the face of a man, of a mortal man against whom Providence had grown as malignant as a mad dog. And the woe upon the face was of such a character that Wolf knew at once that no conceivable social readjustments or ameliorative revolutions could ever atone for it – could ever make up for the simple irremediable fact that it *had* been as it had been![83]

Urging for the state's expiration and Myrddin's Golden Age to arrive before the looming corporate destruction of the environment (part of the frail 'pale blue dot' of Earth, for the popular science writer Carl Sagan), David Goodway has recently suggested that the 'central problem of our time' is 'the imperative to counter irresponsible politicians, bankers and industrialists.'[84] With the G8 countries continuing their pollution of the environment, a report commissioned by 20 states announced in September 2013 that more than 100 million people will die by 2030 if climate change isn't tackled. Reuters elaborated that 'five million deaths occur each year from air pollution, hunger and disease as a result of climate change and carbon-intensive economies, and that toll would likely rise to six million a year by 2030 if current patterns of fossil fuel use continue.' The state-corporate forces which comprise the G8 benefit substantially from this silent genocide, as they do from the deforestation projects in Indonesia and the excessive consumption of the 'developed' nations. The famed UN climate talks are inadequate, writes David Cromwell, 'so long as they do not address the fundamental physical constraints of the Earth's climate system and how to live within them. These constraints and – crucially – how they are under threat by a rampant system of corporate globalisation are taboo subjects for the corporate media.'[85]

David Edwards and David Cromwell, the editors of Media Lens, summarise their views well when they write (concurring with Leopold Bloom's view in *Ulysses* that 'It's the ads and side features [that] sell a weekly not the stale news in the official gazette') in their book *Guardians of Power*:

> In a sane society the extremist 'mainstream' would be considered comical and irrelevant, referenced only for exotic case studies in the human capacity for self-deception in deference to individual and vested self-interest. What is currently considered the alternative media is also misnamed 'the radical media'. In fact it is the *rational* media, rooted in common sense, in genuine rather than merely proclaimed compassion for human suffering, and in a desire to solve problems rather than profit from them.[86]

Writers ranging from Edwards and Cromwell to Chomsky, Edward Herman, Mark Curtis, Jonathan Cook and Greg Philo have emphasized how, like the corporate sector, the elite-leaning views of the media are simply a result of its internal structure and the interests of the dominant powers within it. It should require no discussion to establish that the media have interests of their own which often conflict with the interests of the public. To take a recent example, four days after BBC1 broadcast *The Tax Haven Twins*, John Sweeney's *Panorama* investigation into the *Telegraph*-owning Barclay brothers, the *Telegraph* bit back in a report on December 20th 2012: 'The BBC still needs a lesson in humility. There is little sign in the wake of the Pollard Review that the Jimmy Savile affair has caused the BBC to raise its game.'

Playwright John McGrath aired similar feelings in *A Good Night Out*:

> The gentleman at the head of the powerful opinion-forming corporations do not wish to have their articulate mediation of reality disturbed by a group of people going around with a different story, seeing events from a different perspective, even selecting different information. Still less do they wish to have the population at large emerging from their mental retreat – the inner exile of the powerless and alienated – and demanding a share of power, of control, of freedom.[87]

Many politicians also lobby on behalf of their interests and partners at BP, Chevron, ExxonMobil, Royal Dutch Shell, Edison Electronic Institute, and other firms. Tzeporah Berman writes that 'there are a handful of powerful polluting corporations who are exerting undue influence on the political process to protect their vested interests.'[88] As discussed in earlier chapters, these firms favour short-term profit and ignore long-term consequences, often denying (through lobbying power) that global warming exists at all. Research done by the consultancy firm MM&K and the electronic voting agency Manifest revealed in 2011 that since the turn of the century 'the heads of FTSE 100 firms have seen pay packages quadruple ... even though share prices have not risen during the same period.' Their report warned that 'many companies were shifting away from long-term incentives to annual bonuses, mirroring the approach that caused problems in the banking sector.' The Left Economics Advisory Panel co-ordinator Andrew Fisher commented: 'These figures are yet another display of arrogance from the institutionalised kleptocracy that rules Britain's boardrooms. But such greed is only a symptom of the illness-capitalism. Trade unions should publicise these figures to the millions workers who are told their jobs, pay and pensions are "unaffordable," to show that the money is there, it's just going to someone else.'[89]

Touching on similar concerns, Huxley believed that 'it has now become abundantly clear that the Golden Rule applies not only to the dealings of human individuals and human societies with one another, but also to their dealings with other living creatures and the planet upon which we are all travelling through time and space.'[90] But if the values of obedience and passivity continue to be instilled into the British public through the standard methods of formal education, popular entertainment and the limiting of active citizenship to voting and consuming, then Russell's scintillating words may prove more appropriate:

> After ages during which the earth produced harmless trilobites and butterflies, evolution progressed to the point at which it has generated Neros, Genghis Khans, and Hitlers. This, however, is a passing nightmare; in time the earth will become again incapable of supporting life, and peace will return.[91]

If this vision is to end sooner than Russell expected, it seems all too clear that we must begin to share and serve the interests of the natural environment and all its inhabitants, preparing and sustaining our world, as Porius would insist, not just for later generations, but for the future species that are yet to rise on this lone and 'pale blue dot.'

In *A Glastonbury Romance*, we find the young Rachel Zoyland approving of this suggestion. Positioned atop a fell with the radical poet Ned Athling, she tells him: 'Can't you feel, Ned, as we stand here that this place is magical? What's Poetry if it isn't something that has to fight for the unseen against the seen, for the dead against the living, for the mysterious against the obvious? Poetry always takes sides. It's the only Lost Cause we've got left! It fights for the ... for the ... for the Impossible!'[92]

If the critic John Lucas detected in the Romantic poets the view that 'a poet is the central man of his age and that his responsibilities are therefore enormous,' then Chomsky believes moral responsibility extends much wider.[93] In 'The Responsibility of Intellectuals,' he explained his position on the advantage western intellectuals have in being able to influence the workings of society with their unparalleled resources, and how often this opportunity is wasted, with their time being used instead to be spokesmen of state and corporate power, if occasionally questioning tactics or leadership:

> Intellectuals are in a position to expose the lies of governments, to analyze actions according to their causes and motives and often hidden intentions. In the Western world, at least, they have the power that comes from political liberty, from access to information and freedom of expression. For a privileged minority, Western democracy provides the leisure, the facilities, and the training to seek the truth lying hidden behind the veil of distortion and misrepresentation, ideology and class interest, through which the events of current history are presented to us.[94]

Fred Branfman summarised his views of Chomsky, who he took to Laos in the 1970s during the American bombing raids, in an eloquent piece for *Salon* in June 2012:

> If enough of us had worked like Noam to try to force American leaders to stop killing and exploiting the innocent these past 40 years, after all, countless people would have been saved, and America and the world would not only be far richer, more peaceful and more just. It would not be presently heading toward the collapse of civilization as we know it from

climate change. Noam believes the major responsibility for this lies with a short-term driven corporate system that regards climate change as an 'externality,' i.e., a problem for someone else to worry about. But it is also clear that the fact that not enough of the rest of us, certainly including myself, respond appropriately to civilization's looming death is a major part of the problem as well. And, I thus finally realized, the important question was not why Noam responds the way he does to the suffering of the innocent around the planet. It was why so many of the rest of us do not.[95]

Peter Lavrov, in his *Historical Letters* of 1868 and 1869, likewise believed it was the intelligentsia's responsibility and moral duty to expose the lies and workings of authority, allowing less privileged people to undermine state power themselves. The editors of Media Lens would no doubt agree, since 'to turn a blind eye to our own crimes while focusing on the crimes of others is to guarantee more of both.'[96] Rousseau, in *The Social Contract*, likewise reminded his readers that 'As soon as someone says of the business of the state – "What does it matter to me?" – then the state must be reckoned lost.'[97]

The war guilt, which many already feel from Britain's violent past, has continued to be spread in an effort to bring those who deserve to feel guilty to justice – namely, the principal architects of state, corporate and military power. 'The actual burden,' wrote the early Marx, 'must be made even more burdensome by creating an awareness of it. The humiliation must be increased by making it public. Each sphere of German society must be depicted as the *partie honteuse* of that society and these petrified conditions must be made to dance by having their own tune sung to them! The people must be put in terror of themselves in order to give them courage.'[98] Harold Laski, speaking to a Fabian audience in the autumn of 1947, thought with Marx that most people are less interested in doctrine that in the results of doctrine. We shall be judged, not by the greatness of our purpose, but by the efficiency with which we achieve it. Man is a conservative animal, whose ideas are imprisoned within a framework he is not easily persuaded to abandon ... We are trying to transform a profoundly bourgeois society ... a society, moreover, in which all the major criteria of social values have been imposed by a long indoctrination for whose aid all the power of church and school, of press and cinema and radio, have been very skilfully mobilised; we have got to transform this bourgeois society into a socialist society with foundations not less secure than those it seeks to renovate. We have, moreover, to accomplish this in a dramatically revolutionary period, in which quite literally millions, afraid of the responsibilities of freedom, yearn to cling to whatever they have, however fragmentary, of a security with which they are familiar.[99]

It should be the concern of all to expose the facts about matters of human importance to those who are in a strong position to do something about them. The popular struggles in the Arab world and Latin America, to take the most dramatic examples, should be sources of encouragement for decent people everywhere wishing to bring about changes in their own society. During his speech at the unveiling of Pushkin's monument shortly before his death, Dostoevsky called on the Russian people to 'become a brother of all men, a completely universal man.'[100] But any universal application of human or environmental rights will be hindered, writes David Harvey, so long as we live 'in a world in which the rights of private property and the profit rate trump all other notions of rights.'[101] The formal, (very) partially democratic structures are in place, and have been for decades, which will allow, for example, the outlawing of corporate personhood, or the democratic, nationalised control of certain financial institutions, or which will simply divert public funds from business interests to public infrastructure, such as schools, hospitals, libraries, and other dangerous places of communal activity.

An article most likely written by Élisée Reclus appears to have spread similar sentiments: 'In society today you cannot be considered as an honest man by everybody [sic]. Either you are a robber, assassin and firebrand with the oppressors, the happy and pot-bellied, or you are a robber, assassin and firebrand with the oppressed, the exploited, and the suffering and the underfed. It is up to you, you indecisive and frightened men, to choose. And if you have in your heart the slightest human sentiment, hasten to do so, for at every instant capitalist oppression and exploitation claim new victims, and perpetrate new massacres.'[102] John Stuart Mill rightly pointed out that 'every great movement must experience three stages: ridicule, discussion, adoption.'[103] In countless cases, the importance of educational efforts on the part of local activist movements, often establishing reading groups covering classic anarchist authors, has been a critical factor not only in engaging a wider audience, but also in refining tactics to achieve political or ideological goals. Some invest their intellectual and emotional energy in political party structures, others in extra-parliamentary and environmental movements which seek to 'reclaim the commons.' There is much courage and intelligence in these movements, and all contribute in their own way to deconstructing illegitimate forms of authority, primarily neoliberal structures. Unless these educational and organisational movements are supported, in whatever way our time and energy affords, Ward's anarchist 'seeds beneath the snow' will remain the object of ridicule, and Rosa Luxemburg's 'spiritual transformation' in mankind, which she hoped drastic political change would lead to, will remain purely a thing of literature and art.[104]

Nell Zoyland, in *A Glastonbury Romance*, understands the importance of cultivating these urges in bringing about meaningful change: 'Blind, and dumb, and inarticulate, she felt something surging up within her, that, if she only could express it, would blow all the institutions of the world sky-high.'[105] Paul Trent, the novel's central anarchist, works with Glastonbury's small band of revolutionaries to bring about the establishment of a commune (what he calls 'a voluntary association of free spirits'), though even he, like Luxemburg, understands the limits of his personal political vision, and the ultimately inexplicable, unpredictable nature of social revolution:

> What Paul Trent felt just then was a dim suspicion that if everybody in Glastonbury – these difficult natives as well as these easy visitors – were only to stop doing anything at all, just stop and listen, just stop and grow porous, something far more important than a 'Voluntary Association of Free Spirits' would reveal itself!
>
> A feeling stole over him as if all the way down its long history Glastonbury, the Feminine Person, like Mary at the feet of the Master, had been waiting for the fuss to cease, for the voices to subside, for the dust to sink down.
>
> As when a boy catches upon the face of a girl … that unique feminine look which forever is waiting, listening, dreaming, in a trance of mindless passivity for something that never quite comes, so Paul Trent felt himself now to be watching the Glastonbury atmosphere, on this day of such strange lights and shadows.
>
> Could it be possible that the secret of ecstatic human happiness only arrived, when all outward machinery of life was suspended, all practical activity held in abeyance? Man must live, of course, and children must be born of women; but was there not something else, something more important than any conceivable organization for these great necessary ends?
>
> A doubt came into Paul Trent's mind, different from any he had ever felt, as to whether his inmost ideal – this thing that corresponded to the word liberty – was enough to live by.

Wasn't it only the gap, the space, the vacuum, the hollow and empty no-man's land, into which the fleeting nameless essence could flow and abide? He felt as if he were on the edge of some thrilling secret, as this thought, this doubt, touched him with its breath.[106]

As Trent would be the first to admit, the development of a leaderless, anarchistic revolutionary movement in Britain and other western nations will only be successful if the forces of global interventionism are stymied from inside the imperial powers themselves; a move which would in turn weaken the power of individual states to pass measures (austerity, financial deregulation, privatization) constituting an attack on domestic life. Published in 1933, and later translated into English in 1938, the 'Reflections on War' by the French philosopher and activist Simone Weil declared that 'The great error of nearly all studies of war, an error into which all socialists have fallen, has been to consider war as an episode in foreign politics, when it is especially an act of interior politics, and the most atrocious act of all.'[107]

The question of what anyone who feels powerless can do to dismantle these forms of authority is a timeless one, and superficially appears increasingly difficult, especially in a society which values mental serenity above anything else. As matters currently stand, Goethe's proposal is especially apt: 'We are, and ought to be, obscure to ourselves, turned outwards, and working upon the world which surrounds us.'[108] Hans Blumenberg once said that there must have been a point in human history when we stopped hoping for immortality and instead started to prepare for our great grandchildren. Though the dominant religious, economic and political powers throughout the centuries have attempted to persuade us otherwise, the human race itself is not immortal. For reasons of our fragility, submission to illegitimate authority at this revolutionary stage of human affairs is not an option any of us can afford or risk to take.

Notes

Preface

1. John Cowper Powys, *Porius*, eds. Judith Bond and Morine Krisdóttir (London: Overlook Duckworth, 2007), p. 259.

2. Raymond Williams, *Keywords* (London: Fontana, 1976), p. 37.

3. Alan Moore and David Lloyd, *V for Vendetta* (London: Titan Books, 2005), p. 195.

4. Peter Marshall, *Demanding the Impossible: A History of Anarchism* (London: Harper Perennial, 2008), p. 3.

5. Ephesians 6:12 (NIV).

6. Paul Gibbard, 'Anarchism in English and French Literature, 1885-1914: Zola, the Symbolists, Conrad and Chesterton,' (Oxford D.Phil thesis, 2001).

7. George Woodcock, *Anarchism and Anarchists* (Ontario: Quarry Press, 1992), pp. 78-9.

8. Alex Butterworth, *The World That Never Was: A True Story of Dreamers, Schemers, Anarchists and Secret Agents* (London: Vintage, 2011), p. 171.

9. Patricia Crone, 'Ninth-Century Muslim Anarchists,' *Past and Present*, no. 167, May 2000.

10. Lancelot Hogben to Kingsley Martin, Christmas/New Year 1937/8, cited in C. H. Ralph, *Kingsley: The Life, Letters and Diaries of Kingsley Martin* (London: Gollancz, 1973), pp. 283-4.

11. Peter Kropotkin, *The Conquest of Bread* (Edinburgh: AK Press, 2007), pp. 58-9.

12. Cited in Bryan Palmer, 'The Black and the Red,' *New Left Review* 77, Sept/Oct 2012: 152 (151-60).

13. Marshall, *Demanding the Impossible*, p. 153.

14. Herbert Read, *Poetry and Anarchism* (London: Faber & Faber, 1938), p. 15.

15. David Goodway, *Anarchist Seeds beneath the Snow* (Oakland, CA: PM Press, 2012), p. 8.

16. Chris Hedges, 'Surviving the Fourth of July,' 7 July 2008, *The World As It Is: Dispatches on the Myth of Human Progress* (New York: Nation Books, 2013), pp. 259-60 (pp. 258-63).

17. Paul Thompson, *The Work of William Morris*, 3rd ed. (Oxford University Press, 1991), p. 166.

18. Neil Faulker, 'What is a University Education For?', *The Assault on Universities: A Manifesto for Resistance*, eds. Michael Bailey and Des Freedman (London: Pluto Press, 2011), p. 32.

19. Colin Ward, *Anarchy in Action* (London: Freedom Press, 2008/1973), p. 23.

20. Cited in Laurence J. Peter, *Peter's Quotations* (New York: Bantam Books, 1979), p, 25.

21. Pablo Casals, cited in Inspiration Peak, http://www.inspirationpeak.com/justice.html.

22. Eric Gill, *Last Essays* (London: Jonathan Cape, 1942), p. 55.

23. Simon Nicholson, 'The Theory of Loose Parts: An Important Principle for Design Methodology,' *Studies in Design Education Craft & Technology* 4(2), 1972: 5 (5-14).

1. Occupy Catalonia

1. Sony Lab'ou Tansi, *The Antipeople*, trans. J. A. Underwood (London: Marion Boyars, 1988/1983), p. 28.

2. Immanuel Kant, *The Critique of Practical Reason*, trans. Thomas Kingsmill Abbott, 6th edn. (London: Longmans, Green, and Co., 1927), p. 260.

3. Lindsey German and John Rees, *A People's History of London* (London: Verso, 2012), p. 68.

4. Bertrand Russell, *Proposed Roads to Freedom* (New York: Blue Ribbon Books, 1919), pp. xi-xii.

5. John Dewey, *Experience and Education* (New York:

Touchstone, 1997/1938), p. 21.

6. Emma Goldman, *Anarchism and Other Essays*, pp. 32-33.
7. Gustav Landauer, 'Schwache Stattsmänner, Schwacheres Volk!', *Der Sozialist*, 10 June 1910, trans. in Eugene Lunn, *Prophet of Community: The Romantic Socialism of Gustav Landauer* (University of California Press, 1973), p. 263.
8. Cited in *Chomsky on Anarchism*, ed. Barry Pateman (Edinburgh: AK Press, 2009), p. 103; Peter Kropotkin, 'Anarchism,' *Encyclopædia Britannica* (New York: Encyclopædia Britannica, 1910), vol. 1.
9. Cited in Colin Ward, *Influences: Voices of Creative Dissent* (Bideford: Green Books, 1991), p. 85.
10. Max Weber, *From Max Weber: Essays in Sociology*, trans. Hans Heinrich Gerth and Charles Wright Mills (London: Routledge, 1991), p. 78.
11. Cited in Chris Fitter, *Radical Shakespeare: Politics and Stagecraft in the Early Career* (London: Routledge, 2012), p. 12.
12. Cited in Daniel Guérin, *Anarchism: From Theory to Practice*, trans. Mary Klopper (New York: Monthly Review Press, 1970), p. 12.
13. Immanuel Kant, *The Critique of Practical Reason*, trans. Thomas Kingsmill Abbott, 6th edn. (London: Longmans, Green, and Co., 1927), p. 260.
14. E. P. Thompson, *Witness Against the Beast* (Cambridge University Press, 1994), p. 197; William Blake, *Jerusalem*, 'To the Deists,' in *The Complete Poetry and Prose of William Blake*, ed. David V. Erdman (Berkeley: University of California Press, 1982), p. 202, l. 17-20.
15. Peter Kropotkin, 'In Memory of William Morris,' *Freedom*, November 1896, in Peter Faulkner (ed.), *William Morris: The Critical Heritage* (London: Routledge & Kegan Paul, 1973), p. 400; see, for example, John Goode, 'Now Where Nowhere: William Morris Today,' *News from Nowhere: Journal of*

Cultural Materialism, 9, Autumn 1991: 50-65, and Harry Madgoff, 'The Meaning of Work,' *Monthly Review*, 8(5), October 2006.

16. George Woodcock, *Anarchism* (Harmondsworth: Penguin, 1962), p. 418.

17. William Morris, *News from Nowhere* (London: Longmans, Green, and Co., 1910), p. 77.

18. Ibid.

19. Mark Curtis, *Unpeople: Britain's Secret Human Rights Abuses* (London: Vintage, 2004), pp. 8-9.

20. Cited by Ethan Bronner, *New York Times*, 5 November 2008.

21. Edmund S. Morgan, *Inventing the People: The Rise of Popular Sovereignty in England and America* (London: W. W. Norton & Company, 1989), p. 13 (emphasis his).

22. Stephen Armstrong, *The Road to Wigan Pier Revisited* (London: Constable, 2012), p. 9.

23. Brian Milligan, 'Britain's poorest city: The struggle to make ends meet,' 31 May 2013: http://www.bbc.co.uk/news/business-22623964.

24. Stephen Armstrong, *The Road to Wigan Pier Revisited* (London: Constable, 2012), p. 190.

25. Cited in ibid., p. 220.

26. John Domokos, 'Jobcentres 'tricking' people out of benefits to cut costs, says whistleblower,' 1 April 2011: http://www.theguardian.com/politics/2011/apr/01/jobcentres-tricking-people-benefit-sanctions.

27. Chris Hedges and Joe Sacco, *Days of Destruction, Days of Revolt* (New York: Nation Books, 2012), p. xi.

28. Ibid., p. 13.

29. Ibid., p. 69.

30. Percy Bysshe Shelley, *A Defence of Poetry*.

31. Duncan Wu, ed., *Romanticism: An Anthology*, 3rd edn. (London: Blackwell, 2011), p. 1172.

32. December 15th 1919, cited in F. A. Lea, *Shelley and the*

Romantic Revolution (London: George Routledge & Sons, 1945), p. 358.

33. Audrey Williamson, *Thomas Paine: His Life, Work and Times* (London: George Allen & Unwin, 1973), p. 123.

34. Cited in Percy Bysshe Shelley, *The Mask of Anarchy*, introduced by H. Buxton Forman (London: Reeves and Turner, 1887), p. 5.

35. Richard Seymour, *The Meaning of David Cameron* (Zero Books, 2010), p. 57.

36. Cited in ibid., p. 59.

37. Joseph Stiglitz, 'The fruit of hypocrisy,' *The Guardian*, 16 September 2008.

38. Paul Thompson, *The Work of William Morris*, 3rd edn. (Oxford University Press, 1991), p. 249.

39. Voline, *The Unknown Revolution* (1917-21), in Marshall S. Shatz (ed.), *The Essential Works of Anarchism* (New York: Quadrangle Books, 1972), p. 477.

40. Paul Gallagher, 'Royal wedding invitation to crown prince of Bahrain draws criticism,' *The Guardian*, 23 April 2011.

41. Peter Oborne, 'Cameron deserves better than this ghastly backbench B-team,' *Daily Telegraph*, 20 December 2012.

42. Asa Briggs, 'Introduction,' *William Morris: Selected Writings and Designs*, ed. Asa Briggs (London: Penguin, 1962), pp. 17-8.

43. Ibid., p. 19.

44. Paul Thompson, *The Work of William Morris*, 3rd edn. (Oxford University Press, 1991), p. 207.

45. John Goode, 'William Morris and the Dream of Revolution,' *Politics and Literature in the Nineteenth Century*, ed. John Lucas (London: Methuen, 1971), p. 278.

46. William Morris, 'How I Became a Socialist,' *Justice*, 16 June 1894, in ibid., p. 36.

47. G. D. H. Cole (ed.), *William Morris* (New York: Random House, 1934), p. 374.

48. Harry Pollitt, *Serving My Time* (London: Lawrence and Wishart, 1941), pp. 43-4.
49. Cited in J. T. Murphy, *Preparing for Power* (London: Jonathan Cape, 1934), pp. 75-6.
50. Richard Baxter, *A Holy Commonwealth* (1659), cited in Christopher Hill, *The World Turned Upside Down* (London: Temple Smith, 1972), p. 48, taken from Noam Chomsky, *Deterring Democracy* (London: Vintage, 1992), Chapter 12: Force and Opinion.
51. Robert Crowley, *The Opening of the Wordes of the Prophet Joell*, sigs. F5r-r, cited in David Norbrook, *Poetry and Politics in the English Renaissance* (London: Routledge and Kegan Paul, 1984), p. 53.
52. Andy Wood, *The 1549 Rebellions and the Making of Early Modern England* (Cambridge University Press, 2007), pp. 163-4.
53. Charles Poulson, *The English Rebels* (London: Journeyman, 1984), p. 198.
54. Cited in Hill, *The World Turned Upside Down*.
55. Henry Noel Brailsford, *The Levellers and the English Revolution* (London: Cresset Press, 1961), p. 181.
56. Cited in ibid., p. 64.
57. Ibid., p. 61.
58. Walker, *The Compleat History of Independency*, Part II, p. 156.
59. Cited in Mark Curtis, *Web of Deceit: Britain's Real Role in the World* (London: Vintage, 2003), p. 295.
60. Douglas Jay, *The Socialist Case* (London: Faber and Faber, 1937), p. 317.
61. Hill, *The World Turned Upside Down*, p. 183.
62. Richard Overton, 'To the Right Honourable ... The Commons of England ... The Humble Petition ...', 19 January 1649, in Don M. Wolfe (ed.), *Leveller Manifestoes of the Puritan Revolution* (New York: Thomas Nelson and Sons, 1944), pp. 327-9.

63. Spinoza, *Theologico-Political Treatise*, in *The Chief Works of Benedict de Spinoza*, trans. R. H. M. Elwes (London: G. Bell, 1883 [1670]), vol. 1, p. 258.

64. Ibid., p. 258.

65. Leonard W. Levy, *Emergence of a Free Press* (Oxford University Press, 1985), p. 93.

66. Ibid., p. 94. See also Noam Chomsky, *Deterring Democracy* (London: Vintage, 1992), p. 402.

67. John Milton, *Areopagitica*, in *The Works of John Milton*, gen. ed. Frank A. Patterson, speech ed. William Haller, 18 vols. (Columbia University Press, 1931-38), vol. 4, p. 349.

68. Cited in Herman Ould (ed.), *Freedom of Expression. A Symposium Based on the Conference called by the London Centre of the International P.E.N. to Commemorate the Tercentenary of the Publication of Milton's Areopagitica, 22-26th August, 1944* (London: Hutchinson International Authors, 1944), p. 78, as cited in Levy, p. 94.

69. Cited in G. E. M. De Ste Croix, *The Class Struggle in the Ancient Greek World: From the Archaic Age to the Arab Conquests* (Cornell University Press, 1981), p. 355.

70. P. Boitani, 'Chaucer's Labyrinth: Fourteenth-Century Literature and Language,' *The Chaucer Review* 17(3), Winter 1983: 202.

71. Benson, L. (ed.), *The Riverside Chaucer*, 3rd edn. (Oxford University Press, 2008), p. 358, l. 878.

72. Cited in Hill, *The World Turned Upside Down*, p. 16.

73. Cited in Maurice Ashley, *Life in Stuart England* (London: B. T. Batsford, 1964), pp. 21-2.

74. Joseph Beaumont, *Psyche: Or Loves Mysterie*, in *The Complete Poems of Dr. Joseph Beaumont (1615-1699)*, ed. Alexander Balloch Grosart (New York: AMS Press,1967), vol. 2, p. 67.

75. George Orwell, *Homage to Catalonia* (London: Penguin, 2000), pp. 88, 3.

76. Ibid., pp. 57, 88.

77. Ibid., p. 59.
78. Ibid., p. 87.
79. Ibid., p. 7.
80. Ibid., pp. 28-9.
81. Victor Serge, *From Lenin to Stalin*, trans. Ralph Manheim, 2nd ed. (London: Pathfinder, 1972), p. 125.
82. Orwell, *Homage to Catalonia*, p. 109.
83. George Orwell, *Inside the Whale* (1940), 'Charles Dickens.'
84. Peter Kropotkin, *The Conquest of Bread*.
85. Cited in Daniel Guérin, *Anarchism: From Theory to Practice*, trans. Mary Klopper (New York: Monthly Review Press, 1970), p. 78.
86. Murray Bookchin, *Social Anarchism or Lifestyle Anarchism: An Unbridgeable Chasm?* (Edinburgh: AK Press, 1995), pp. 9-10.
87. Mark Fisher, 'Exiting the Vampire Castle', 22 November 2013, *The North Star*: http://www.thenorthstar.info/?p=11 299.
88. Ibid., p. 211.
89. Ibid., p. 202.
90. Chris Harman, *A People's History of the World: From the Stone Age to the New Millennium* (London: Verso, 2008), p. 522.
91. Cited in Chomsky, 'Objectivity and Liberal Scholarship,' *Chomsky on Anarchism*, ed. Barry Pateman (Edinburgh: AK Press, 2009), p. 70.
92. Cited in John Darwin, *The Empire Project: The Rise and Fall of the British World-System, 1830-1970* (Cambridge University Press, 2009), p. 268.
93. G. A. Stone, *Spain, Portugal and the Great Powers, 1931-1941* (Houndmills, Basingstoke: Palgrave Macmillan, 2005), p. 148.
94. Richard Wigg, *Churchill and Spain: The Survival of the Franco Regime, 1940-1945* (Oxford University Press, 2005), p. 153.
95. Danny Gluckstein, *A People's History of the Second World*

War: Resistance versus Empire (London: Pluto Press, 2012), p. 16.

96. V. I. Lenin, *State and Revolution* (New York: International Publishers, 1932), pp. 39-40; Shatz, *The Essential Works of Anarchism*, p. 539.

97. 'Collectivisation Decree of Catalonia,' 24 December 1936, cited in Gluckstein, *A People's History of the Second World War*, p. 16.

98. Daniel Guérin, *Anarchism: From Theory to Practice*, trans. Mary Klopper (New York: Monthly Review Press, 1970), pp. 131-3.

99. Chomsky, 'Objectivity and Liberal Scholarship,' *Chomsky on Anarchism*, p. 73.

100. Karl Marx and Friedrich Engels, *The Communist Manifesto* (Middlesex: Echo Library, 2009), p. 34.

101. Orwell, *Homage to Catalonia*, pp. 186-7.

102. Augustin Souchy, *Beware! Anarchist: A Life for Freedom*, trans. Theo Waldinger, ed. Sam Dolgoff and Richard Ellington (Chicago: Charles H. Kerr, 1992 [1977]), ch. 11.

103. *Collectivisations: l'oeuvre constructive de la revolution espagnole*, 2nd ed. (Toulouse, Editions C.N.T., 1965), cited in Chomsky, 'Objectivity and Liberal Scholarship,' *Chomsky on Anarchism*, p. 73.

104. Cited in Sam Dolgoff, *The Anarchist Collectives: Workers' Self-Management in the Spanish Revolution, 1936-1939* (New York: Black Rose Books, 1974), p. 6.

105. George Orwell, *The Road to Wigan Pier* (London: Penguin, 2001), pp. 207-8.

106. Ibid., p. x.

107. Ibid., p. 6.

108. Ibid., p. 12.

109. Ibid., p. 12.

110. Ibid., p. 68 (emphasis his).

111. Ibid., p. 117.

112. Loraine Saunders, *The Unsung Artistry of George Orwell* (London: Ashgate, 2008), p. 24; Jenni Calder, *Chronicles of Conscience: A Study of George Orwell and Arthur Koestler* (Pittsburgh: University of Pittsburgh Press, 1968), p. 43.

113. Orwell, *The Road to Wigan Pier*, p. 128.

114. Ibid., p. 14.

115. Ibid., p. 15.

116. Ibid., p. 164.

117. Ibid., p. 18.

118. Ibid., p. 18.

119. Ibid., p. 20.

120. Ibid., p. 32.

121. Ibid., p. 29.

122. Ibid., p. 29.

123. Ibid., p. 30.

124. Ibid.

125. Ibid., p. 35.

126. Karl Marx, *Critique of the Gotha Programme*, in *Karl Marx and Friedrich Engels Selected Works*, vol. II (Moscow: Foreign Languages Publishing House), p. 25.

127. Orwell, *The Road to Wigan Pier*, pp. 25-6.

128. Ibid., p. 38, 34.

129. Ibid., p. 44 (emphasis his).

130. Ibid., p. 52.

2. This Side of Paradise

1. Speech at Birmingham and Midland Institute, 27 September 1869, in K. J. Fielding (ed.), *Speeches of Charles Dickens* (Oxford: Clarendon, 1960).

2. David Bradshaw (ed.), *The Hidden Huxley* (London: Faber & Faber, 1994), pp. viii-ix.

3. Aldous Huxley, *Proper Studies: The Proper Study of Mankind is Man* (London: Chatto & Windus, 1927), pp. 272-82.

4. Aldous Huxley, *Ends and Means* (London: Chatto & Windus,

1949), pp. 3, 70.

5. Aldous Huxley, *After Many a Summer* (London: Chatto & Windus, 1939).

6. Grover Smith (ed.), *Letters of Aldous Huxley* (London: Chatto & Windus, 1969), p. 944; Marshall, *Demanding the Impossible*, p. 570.

7. Goldman Archive, International Institute of Social History, Amsterdam, VI, letter from Huxley to Emma Goldman, 15 March 1938.

8. Aldous Huxley, *Island* (London: Flamingo, 1994), pp. 82, 84.

9. Ibid., p. 165.

10. Ibid., p. 105.

11. Ibid., p. 161.

12. William Morris, 'Monopoly; or, How Labour is Robbed': http://www.marxists.org/archive/morris/works/1890/monop oly.htm.

13. Cited in *The Cambridge Companion to Chomsky*, ed. James McGilvray (Cambridge University Press, 2005), p. 233.

14. Joshua Hagler, *The Boy Who Made Silence* (Hertfordshire: Markasia Enterprises, 2012); May Morris, *William Morris: Artist, Writer, Socialist*, vol. I (Oxford: Blackwell, 2 vols., 1936), pp. 292-3.

15. John Ruskin, *The Stones of Venice*, vol. II (New York: Merrill & Baker, 3 vols., 1851-3), pp. 161-2.

16. Huxley, *Island*, p. 162.

17. Aldous Huxley, *The Doors of Perception and Heaven and Hell* (London: Flamingo, 1994 [1954]), p. 52.

18. Cited in Alex Butterworth, *The World That Never Was: A True Story of Dreamers, Schemers, Anarchists and Secret Agents* (London: Vintage, 2011), p. 91.

19. David Foster Wallace, *Infinite Jest* (London: Abacus, 1997), p. 154; Paulo Freire, *The Politics of Education: Culture, Power, and Liberation*, cited in Noam Chomsky, *Chomsky on MisEducation*, ed. Donaldo Macedo (New York: Rowman &

Littlefield, 2000), pp. 19-20.

20. F. Burkhardt (ed.), *Charles Darwin's Letters: A Selection* (Cambridge University Press, 1996), p. 99.

21. Giovanni Pico della Mirandola, *Oration on the Dignity of Man*, trans. A. R. Capongiri (Chicago: Gateway, 1956), p. 7.

22. Laurence Davis, 'Introduction,' *The New Utopian Politics of Ursula K. Le Guin's The Dispossessed* [*TNUP*], ed. Laurence Davis and Peter Stillman (London: Lexington Books, 2005), p. ix.

23. Dan Sabia, 'Individual and Community in Le Guin's *The Dispossessed*,' ibid., p. 111.

24. Ursula Le Guin, *The Dispossessed* (New York: Avon, 1975), p. 1.

25. Ibid., p. 12.

26. Ibid., p. 103.

27. *Is the Man Who Is Tall Happy?: An Animated Conversation with Noam Chomsky*, dir. Michel Gondry, Partizan Films, 2013.

28. Cited in Robert F. Barsky, *Noam Chomsky: A Life of Dissent* (Cambridge, MA.: MIT Press, 1997), p. 15.

29. Le Guin, *The Dispossessed*, p. 104.

30. Ibid., p. 118.

31. Ibid., p. 117.

32. Cited in Noam Chomsky, 'Democracy and Education,' Mellon Lecture, Loyola University, Chicago, 19 October 1994, www.e-text.org/text/Chomsky%20Noam%20-%20Democracy%20and%20Education.txt.

33. Alex Butterworth, *The World That Never Was: A True Story of Dreamers, Schemers, Anarchists and Secret Agents* (London: Vintage, 2011), p. 105.

34. Peter Kropotkin, *Memoirs of a Revolutionist* (1899), in Marshall S. Shatz (ed.), *The Essential Works of Anarchism* (New York: Quadrangle Books, 1972), p. 310 (emphasis his).

35. Le Guin, *The Dispossessed*, p. 13.

36. Ibid., p. 19.

37. Ibid., p. 52.
38. Noam Chomsky, 'Destroying the Commons,' 22 July 2012, http://chomsky.info/articles/20120722.htm; Le Guin, *The Dispossessed*, pp. 112, 163.
39. Chris Hedges, 'The False Idol of Unfettered Capitalism,' 15 March 2009, *The World As It Is: Dispatches on the Myth of Human Progress* (New York: Nation Books, 2013), p. 12 (pp. 8-13).
40. Erich Fromm, *The Art of Loving* (London: HarperPerennial, 1956/2006), pp. 80-1.
41. Terry Eagleton, *The Function of Criticism* (London: Verso, 1984), p. 122.
42. Chris Hedges and Joe Sacco, *Days of Destruction, Days of Revolt* (New York: Nation Books, 2012), p. 238.
43. Eddie Izzard, 'Brilliant Britain': www.youtube.com /watch?v=oZDreHPzU94.
44. Interview with Woody Harrelson by Rob Tannenbaum, *Details*, June/July 2013: http://www.details.com/celebrities-entertainment/movies-and-tv/201306/woody-harrelson-game-change-hunger-games-sequel-films#/ixzz2UtGCIWMY.
45. Cited in Sharon Beder, *Global Spin: The Corporate Assault on Environmentalism* (Devon: Green Books, 1997), p. 163.
46. David Edwards and David Cromwell, *Guardians of Power: The Myth of the Liberal Media* (London: Pluto, 2006), p. 209.
47. Lucy Ward, 'Doubt and Depression Burden Teenage Girls,' *The Guardian*, 24 February 2005.
48. Le Guin, *The Dispossessed*, p. 105.
49. Ibid., p. 120.
50. Ibid., p. 121.
51. Ibid., p. 112.
52. Morris, *News from Nowhere*, p. 89.
53. Ibid., 128.
54. Winterson, 'Breaching Invisible Walls,' *TNUP*, p. 150.

55. Le Guin, *The Dispossessed*, p. 136; Philip K. Dick, 'The Last of the Masters,' *The Philip K. Dick Reader* (New York: Citadel Press, 1997); J. M Coetzee, *The Childhood of Jesus* (London: Harvill Secker, 2013).
56. Laurence Davis, 'The Dynamic and Revolutionary Utopia of Ursula K. Le Guin,' *TNUP*, p. 10.
57. Le Guin, *The Dispossessed*, p. 197.
58. Ibid., p. 267.
59. Lemony Snicket, *Who Could That Be at This Hour?*, All the Wrong Questions 1 (London: Egmont, 2012); Lemony Snicket, *When Did You See Her Last?*, All the Wrong Questions 2 (London: Egmont, 2013).

3. Atheists, Statists, and the English Literati

1. The following section is an extended version of an essay published online by *Ceasefire Magazine*, 'Review: Unhitched: The Trial of Christopher Hitchens by Richard Seymour,' 3 February 2013.
2. Richard Seymour, *Unhitched: The Trial of Christopher Hitchens* (London: Verso, 2012), p. xlv.
3. Glenn Greenwald, 'Christopher Hitchens and the protocol for public figure deaths,' 17 December 2011, *Salon*.
4. Seymour, *Unhitched*, p. 67.
5. T. B. Bottomore (ed.), *Karl Marx: Early Writings* (London: C. A. Warrs, 1963), p. 44.
6. Pierre Corneille, *Horace* (1640), act II, scene viii.
7. Matthew 22:21 (NIV).
8. F. B. Smith, *The Making of the Second Reform Bill* (London, 1966), pp. 24-5.
9. Christopher Hill, *The World Turned Upside Down* (London: Temple Smith, 1972), p. 122.
10. Mikhail Bakunin, in Marshall S. Shatz (ed.), *The Essential Works of Anarchism* (New York: Quadrangle Books, 1972), p. 133.

11. Alan Sokal, *Beyond the Hoax: Science, Philosophy and Culture* (Oxford University Press, 2008), p. 453.

12. Adrian Mitchell, *Poems* (London: Jonathan Cape, 1964), p. 8; Eagleton, *Red Pepper*, October 2008.

13. Bryan Scott, 'Stephen Fry's Olympics open letter was a masterclass in eloquence,' 8 August 2013, *Metro*: http://metro.co.uk/2013/08/08/stephen-frys-olympics-open-letter-was-a-masterclass-in-eloquence-3916192/.

14. Stephen Fry, 'An Open Letter to David Cameron and the IOC,' 7 August 2013: http://www.stephenfry.com/2013/08/07/an-open-letter-to-david-cameron-and-the-ioc/single-page; Glenn Greenwald, 'Sam Harris, the New Atheists, and anti-Muslim animus,' 3 April 2013, *Guardian*: http://www.theguardian.com/commentisfree/2013/apr/03/sam-harris-muslim-animus.

15. Nicholas Watt, 'Enigma codebreaker Alan Turing to be given posthumous pardon,' 19 July 2013, *Guardian*: http://www.theguardian.com/uk-news/2013/jul/19/enigma-codebreaker-alan-turing-posthumous-pardon.

16. Ashok Kumar, 'Want to cleanse your city of its poor? Host the Olympics,' 12 April 2012, *Ceasefire Magazine*: http://ceasefiremagazine.co.uk/olympics-opportunity-cleanse-city.

17. http://www.youtube.com/watch?v=JUzpLFKb-qA.

18. Chris Hedges, *I Don't Believe in Atheists* (London: Continuum, 2008), p. 84.

19. Seymour, *Unhitched*, p. 6.

20. Ibid., p. 34.

21. Ibid., p. 37.

22. Ibid., p. 42.

23. Ibid., p. 54.

24. Ibid.

25. Ibid., p. 55.

26. Cited in ibid., p. 60.

27. David Webster, *Dispirited: How Contemporary Spirituality*

Makes Us Stupid, Selfish and Unhappy (Winchester: Zero Books, 2012), p. 7.

28. Seymour, *Unhitched*, p. 61.
29. Ibid., p. 62.
30. Ruth Kinna, *Anarchism: A Beginner's Guide* (Oxford: Oneworld Publications, 2009), p. 62; ibid.
31. Cited in Seymour, *Unhitched*, p. 63.
32. Glenn Greenwald, 'Sam Harris, the New Atheists, and anti-Muslim animus,' 3 April 2013, *Guardian*: http://www.theguardian.com/commentisfree/2013/apr/03/sam-harris-muslim-animus.
33. Seymour, *Unhitched*, p. 71.
34. Moshe Adler, *Economics for the Rest of Us: Debunking the Science that Makes Life Dismal* (London: The New Press, 2010), p. 192.
35. Cited in Edward Herman, *Beyond Hypocrisy: Decoding the News in an Age of Propaganda* (Cambridge, MA: South End Press, 1992), p. 17.
36. Cited in Dan Jellinek, *People Power: A User's Guide to Democracy* (London: Bantam Press, 2013), p. 154.
37. Cited in Heather Brooke, *The Silent State* (London: Windmill Books, 2011), p. 240.
38. Gerrard Winstanley, *The Law of Freedom* (1652), in G. H. Sabine (ed.), *The Works of Gerrard Winstanley* (Cornell University Press, 1941), p. 577.
39. John Gray, *Straw Dogs: Thoughts on Humans and Other Animals* (London: Granta Books, 2002), p. xi.
40. Ibid., p. 92.
41. Cited in Seymour, *Unhitched*, p. xvi.
42. Ibid., p. 98.
43. Ibid., p. xxii.
44. Ibid., p. 17.

4. Workers and Writers

1. The following section is an extended version of an essay published online by *Ceasefire Magazine*, 'Review: "The Intellectual Life of the British Working Classes" by Jonathan Rose,' 3 April 2013; Antoine de Saint Exupéry, *The Little Prince*, (New York: Reynal and Hitchcock, 1943).

2. Ludwig Wittgenstein, *Culture and Value*, trans. Peter Winch, ed. G. H. von Wright (Chicago University Press, 1977), p. 54.

3. Jonathan Rose, *The Intellectual Life of the British Working Classes*, 2nd edition (Yale University Press, 2010), p. 395.

4. Ibid., p. 393.

5. Virginia Woolf, *A Writer's Diary*, p. 47.

6. Rose, *The Intellectual Life of the British Working Classes*, p. 393.

7. T. S. Eliot, *After Strange Gods* (London: Faber & Faber, 1934), pp. 19-20.

8. Rose, *The Intellectual Life of the British Working Classes*, p. 223.

9. Ibid., p. 438.

10. Ibid., p. 223.

11. Cited in ibid., p. 224; Bernard Capp, *The World of John Taylor the Water-Poet* (Oxford: Clarendon Press, 1994).

12. Cited in ibid., p. 15.

13. Cited in David E. Martin and David Rubinstein (eds.), *Ideology and the Labour Movement: Essays Presented to John Saville* (London: Croom Helm, 1979), pp. 33-4.

14. Anthony O'Reilly, Independent News & Media Plc Annual Report 2004, p. 3.

15. Cited in Elizabeth Fones-Wolf, *Selling Free Enterprise* (University of Illinois Press, 1994), p. 45.

16. Raymond Kuhn, *Politics and the Media in Britain* (New York: Palgrave Macmillan, 2007), p. 32.

17. Ibid., p. 6.

18. Rose, *The Intellectual Life of the British Working Classes*, p. 58.

19. Daniel and Gabriel Cohn-Bendit, *Obsolete Communism: The Left-Wing Alternative* (New York: McGraw Hill, 1968), p. 554.

20. Peter Davidson (ed.), *The Lost Orwell: Being a Supplement to 'The Complete Work of Orwell'* (London: Timewell Press, 2006), p. 116.

21. Rose, *The Intellectual Life of the British Working Classes*, p. 149.

22. John Dewey, *Experience and Education* (New York: Touchstone, 1997/1938), pp. 46, 49.

23. Rose, *The Intellectual Life of the British Working Classes*, p. 294.

24. Ibid., p. 283.

25. John Holt, *How Children Fail* (New York: Pitman Publishing Company, 1964).

26. Thomas Huxley, *Science and Education*, vol. III of *Collected Essays* (New York: Greenwood Press, 1968), p. 86.

27. Ibid., p. 83.

28. Ibid., p. 101.

29. Cited in Noam Chomsky, *Chomsky on Democracy & Education*, ed. C. P. Otero (London: Routledge, 2003), p. 2.

30. Bertrand Russell, *Proposed Roads to Freedom – Anarchy, Socialism and Syndicalism* (New York: Henry Holt & Co., 1919), pp. 186-7.

31. Cited in Ruth Kinna, *Anarchism: A Beginner's Guide* (Oxford: Oneworld Publications, 2009), p. 46.

32. Isaac Newton, in Joseph Spence, *Observations, Anecdotes, and Characters of Books and Men*, ed. J. M. Osborn (Oxford: Clarendon Press, 1966), no. 1259.

33. Stephen Bayley, 'There's a Lesson in all this,' *Observer*, 13 July 2008.

34. Graeme Paton, 'Exam factory approach "damaging education",' *Daily Telegraph*, 23 August 2013; John Dewey, 'Democracy and Education in the World Today,' 1938, *Problems of Men* (New York: Philosophical Library, 1946), p. 36.

35. Terry Eagleton, 'Death of the intellectual,' *Red Pepper*, October 2008.

36. Norman Fairclough, *Discourse and Social Change*

(Cambridge: Polity Press, 1992).

37. Owen Hatherley, *A Guide to the New Ruins of Great Britain* (London: Verso, 2010), pp. 72-3.

38. Ibid., pp. 64-5.

39. Ibid., p. 132.

40. Ibid., p. 339.

41. Ibid., p. 342.

42. Ibid., pp. 349-50.

43. Paul and Percival Goodman, *Communitas: Means of Livelihood and Ways of Life*, p. 597.

44. David Harvey, 'The Right to the City,' *New Left Review*, vol. 53, September-October 2008, p. 32.

45. For related issues, see my 'Student activism on campus', *Impact Magazine*, September 2012: http://www.impactnottingham.com/2012/09/student-activism-on-campus/; http://issuu.com/impact_magazine/docs/issue_218_for_web

46. Joel Bakan, *The Corporation: The Pathological Pursuit of Profit and Power* (London: Constable, 2004), p. 50.

47. Dinyar Godrej, 'A healthy mind in a healthy society,' *New Internationalist*, May 2012.

48. *Economist*, 26 March 2011.

49. Bakan, *The Corporation*, p. 69.

50. Robert Reich, 'How not to change big pharma', *Salon*, 5 July 2012: http://www.salon.com/2012/07/05/how_not_to_change_big_pharma_salpart.

51. 'Sir David Attenborough's Response, Conferment of Distinguished Honorary Fellowships, University of Leicester Graduation Ceremony, 10/07/2006': http://www.youtube.com/watch?v=5OEdKWrJewY.

52. James Wilson, 'The individual, the state, and the corporation,' *The Cambridge Companion to Chomsky*, ed. James McGilvray (Cambridge University Press, 2005), p. 247.

53. Cited in David E. Martin and David Rubinstein (eds.), *Ideology and the Labour* Movement: Essays Presented to John

Saville (London: Croom Helm, 1979), p. 51.

54. Rudolf Rocker, *Anarcho-Syndicalism: Theory and Practice* (AK Press, 2004), ch. 4.

55. Cited in Ralph Miliband, *Capitalist Democracy in Britain* (Oxford University Press, 1982), p. 22, n. 2.

56. *Economist*, 21 November 1846, cited in Asa Briggs, 'The Language of 'Mass' and 'Masses' in Nineteenth-Century England,' in Martin and Rubinstein, *Ideology and the Labour Movement*, p. 76.

57. Cited in David E. Martin and David Rubinstein (eds.), *Ideology and the Labour Movement: Essays Presented to John Saville* (London: Croom Helm, 1979), p. 249.

58. Cited in ibid., p. 49.

59. Cited in Richard Seymour, *The Meaning of David Cameron* (Zero Books, 2010), p. 22.

60. 'Political Discourse and the Propaganda System,' 24 October 1986, from Chomsky, *Language and Politics*, pp. 558-9.

61. Cited in Robin Hahnel, *Economic Justice and Democracy: From Competition to Cooperation* (London: Routledge, 2005), p. 216.

62. George Orwell, *Inside the Whale* (1940), 'Charles Dickens.'

63. Peter Kropotkin, *The Conquest of Bread*.

64. Cited in Daniel Guérin, *Anarchism: From Theory to Practice*, trans. Mary Klopper (New York: Monthly Review Press, 1970), p. 78.

65. Murray Bookchin, *Social Anarchism or Lifestyle Anarchism: An Unbridgeable Chasm?* (Edinburgh: AK Press, 1995), pp. 9-10.

66. David Harvey, *A Brief History of Neoliberalism* (Oxford University Press, 2005), p. 119.

67. Leo Tolstoy, *The Kingdom of God Is Within You* (1894), in Marshall S. Shatz (ed.), *The Essential Works of Anarchism* (New York: Quadrangle Books, 1972), p. 261.

68. Ralph Cudworth, *The True Intellectual System of the Universe*,

(Gould & Newman, 1837 [1678]), Preface, p. 35.

69. Danny Dorling, *So You Think You Know About Britain?* (London: Constable, 2011), p. 231.

70. Bakan, *The Corporation*, p. 37.

71. *There Will Be Blood*, dir. Paul Thomas Anderson, Miramax Films, 2007.

72. *The Master*, dir. Paul Thomas Anderson, Annapurna Pictures, 2012.

73. Des Freedman, 'An Introduction to Education Reform and Resistance,' *The Assault on Universities: A Manifesto for Resistance*, ed. Michael Bailey and Des Freedman (London: Pluto Press, 2011), p. 5.

74. Richard Van Noorden, 'UK government warned over 'catastrophic' cuts,' *Nature*, vol. 466, pp. 420-421 (2010).

75. Peter Scott, 'And so farewell to my 'stakeholders,'' *Education Guardian*, 22 February 2011, cited in Ibid.

76. Bertrand Russell, 'On the Notion of Cause,' *Proceedings of the Aristotelian Society*, 13: 1 (1-26).

77. Judith Suissa, *Anarchism and Education: A Philosophical Perspective* (Oakland: PM Press, 2010), p. 77.

78. P. Avrich, *The Modern School Movement: Anarchism and Education in the United States* (Princeton University Press, 1980), p. 20.

79. Fransisco Ferrer y Guardia, *The Origin and Ideals of the Modern School* (London: Watts, 1913), p. 55.

80. Ibid.

81. Colin Ward, *Anarchy in Action* (London: Freedom Press, 2008/1973).

82. Cited in George Woodcock, *Anarchism and Anarchists* (Ontario: Quarry Press, 1992), p. 207.

83. 'Ken Robinson says schools kill creativity,' TED 2006, February: www.ted.com/talks/lang/eng/ken_robinson_says_schools_kill_creativity.html.

84. Cited in Colin Ward, *Talking Anarchy*, with David Goodway

(London: Freedom Press, 2003), p. 93.

85. Heather Brooke, *The Silent State* (London: Windmill Books, 2011), p.88.

86. David Hay and Rebecca Nye, *The Spirit of the Child* (London: Jessica Kingsley Publishers, 2006).

87. Rose, *The Intellectual Life of the British Working Classes*, p. 185.

88. Ibid., p. 190.

89. Ibid., p. 123.

90. Ibid., p. 82.

91. Ibid., p. 187.

92. Ibid., p. 145.

93. Ibid., p. 464.

94. Richard Gott, *Britain's Empire: Resistance, Repression and Revolt* (London: Verso, 2011), p. 8.

95. Rose, *The Intellectual Life of the British Working Classes*, p. 464.

96. William Paul, *The State: Its Origin and Function* (Glasgow: Socialist Labour Press, 1917), pp. 197-8.

97. Rose, *The Intellectual Life of the British Working Classes*, p. 51.

98. Ibid., p. 37.

99. Ibid., pp. 55, 393.

100. Ibid., pp. 55-6.

101. Ibid., p. 56.

102. Susan Watkins, 'Presentism? A Reply to T. J. Clark,' *New Left Review* 74, March/April2012: 78 (77-102).

103. Rose, *The Intellectual Life of the British Working Classes*, p. 350.

104. Ibid., p. 352.

105. J. M. Coetzee, *Slow Man* (London: Vintage, 2006), p. 64.

106. Rose, *The Intellectual Life of the British Working Classes*, p. 402.

107. Ibid., p. 40.

108. Ibid., p. 111.

109. Cited in Laurence J. Peter, *Peter's Quotations* (New York: Bantam Books, 1979), p, 25.

5. Nothing to Declare?

1. Alan Moore, J. H. Williams III, and Mick Gray, *Absolute Promethea: Book One* (La Jolla, CA.: WildStorm, 2009), ch. 5, 'Weapon for Liberty.'
2. Ibid.
3. Alan Grant, Norm Breyfogle and Josef Rubinstein, *Batman: Anarky* (London: Titan Book, 1999), 'Introduction' by Alan Grant.
4. Ibid., p. 9.
5. Ibid., p. 119.
6. Le Guin, The Dispossessed, p. 103.
7. Edward Carpenter, *Toward Democracy* (London: Allen & Unwin, 1918), p. 58.
8. Percival W. H. Almy, 'New Views of Mr Oscar Wilde,' *The Theatre*, XXIII, March 1894, in E. H. Mikhail (ed.), *Oscar Wilde*, vol. 1 (London: Macmillan, 1979), p. 232.
9. Thomas Bell, 'Oscar Wilde without Whitewash' (typescript, c. 1935-8, William Andrews Clark Memorial Library, University of California), p. 93.
10. Letter from Kropotkin to Robert Ross, 6 May 1905, in Margery Ross (ed.), *Robert Ross, Friend of Friends: Letters to Robert Ross, Art Critic and Writer, Together with Extracts from His Published Articles* (London: Jonathan Cape, 1952), p. 113.
11. Cited in Jerusha McCormack, 'Wilde's fiction(s),' *The Cambridge Companion to Oscar Wilde*, ed. Peter Raby (Cambridge University Press, 1997), p.101.
12. Peter Marshall, *Demanding the Impossible: A History of Anarchism* (London: Harper Perennial, 2008), p. 163.
13. Letter from Kropotkin to Robert Ross, 6 May 1905, in Margery Ross (ed.), *Robert Ross, Friend of Friends* (London: Jonathan Cape, 1952), p. 113.
14. Marshall, *Demanding the Impossible*, p. 180.
15. Owen Dudley Edwards, 'Wilde, Oscar Fingal O'Flahertie Wills (1854–1900),' *Oxford Dictionary of National Biography*

(Oxford University Press, 2004); online edn., Sept 2012, http://www.oxforddnb.com/view/article/29400.

16. David Hume, 'Of the First Principles of Government,' *Essays: Moral, Political, and Literary*, ed. Eugene F. Miller (Indianapolis: Liberty Fund, 1985), p. 34 (pp. 32-6).

17. Peter Davidson (ed.), *The Complete Works of George Orwell* (London: Secker & Warburg, 1998), vol. 19, p. 157.

18. Thomas Bell, 'Oscar Wilde's Unwritten Play,' *The Bookman*, April-May 1930, p. 141.

19. Oscar Wilde, 'The Soul of Man Under Socialism' ['SOM'], in Richard Ellmann (ed.), *The Artist as Critic* (New York: Random House, 1969), p. 258.

20. Thomas Bell, 'Oscar Wilde without Whitewash' (William Andrews Clark Memorial Library, University of California, typescript c. 1935-8), p. 93.

21. Wilde, 'SOM', in Ellmann, *Artist as Critic*.

22. *The Cambridge Companion to Oscar Wilde*, ed. Peter Raby (Cambridge University Press, 1997).

23. Wilde, 'SOM,' in Ellmann, *Artist as Critic*, p. 258.

24. Anonymous, 'What it is like to be a girl in an anarchist boys club': http://www.spunk.org/texts/anarcfem/sp000168.html.

25. Oscar Wilde, *A Woman of No Importance*, in *Complete Works of Oscar Wilde* (London: Collins, 1966), p. 437.

26. Wilde, 'SOM,' p. 258.

27. *Oscar Wilde: The Critical Heritage*, ed. Karl Beckson (London: Routledge, 1970), pp. 114-5; Oscar Wilde, 'The Young King,' *Complete Works of Oscar Wilde* (London: Harper Collins, 1994), p. 216.

28. Wilde, 'SOM,' p. 266.

29. Oscar Wilde, 'The Ballad of Reading Gaol,' in Bobby Fong and Karl Beckson (eds.), *The Complete Works of Oscar Wilde*, vol. 1 (Oxford University Press, 2000), p. 213.

30. Wilde, 'SOM,' p. 282.

31. Ibid., p. 284.

32. Peter Kropotkin, *The Conquest of Bread.*
33. Cited in Alex Butterworth, *The World That Never Was: A True Story of Dreamers, Schemers, Anarchists and Secret Agents* (London: Vintage, 2011), p. 34.
34. Cited in ibid., p. 79.
35. Ibid., pp. 38-9.
36. *Peace News,* 20 February 1959, cited in Colin Ward, *Anarchy in Action* (London: Freedom Press, 2008/1973), p. 46.
37. Bertrand Russell, 'My Religious Reminiscences,' *The Basic Writings of Bertrand Russell, 1903-1959,* eds. Robert E. Egner and Lester E. Dennon (London: Routledge, 1999), p. 36.
38. Oscar Wilde, 'A Chinese Sage,' *Speaker,* 8 February 1890, in Ellmann, *Artist as Critic,* pp. 223-5.
39. Wilde, 'SOM'.
40. Ibid.
41. Butterworth, *The World That Never Was,* p. 105.
42. Kropotkin, *The Essential Anarchism,* p. 310 (emphasis his).
43. Paulo Freire and Donaldo Macedo, *Literacy: Reading the Word and the World* (South Hadley, Mass.: Bergin & Garvey, 1987), p. 32.
44. Harman, *A People's History of the World,* p. ii.
45. Ibid., p. iii.
46. Godwin, *The Essential Works of Anarchism,* p. 9.
47. Noam Chomsky, 'Objectivity and Liberal Scholarship,' *Chomsky on Anarchism,* ed. Barry Pateman (Edinburgh: AK Press, 2009), p. 13.

6. Intellectual Nonsense and the Fear of Rationality

1. The following section is an extended version of an essay which appeared online on *Anarchist News,* 18 February 2013; Letter to Robert Egner, 27 June 1955, *The Selected Letters of Bertrand Russell: The Public Years, 1914-1970,* ed. Nicholas Griffin (London: Routledge, 2001), p. 593.
2. Mary Douglas and Baron Isherwood, *The World of Goods:*

Towards and Anthropology of Consumption (London: Routledge, 1996).

3. Andrew Hadfield, *Shakespeare and Republicanism* (Cambridge University Press, 2008), p. 7.

4. AAAS Press Room, 'Evolution on the Front Line,' http://www.aaas.org/news/press_room/evolution/qanda.sh tml

5. Peter Medawar, 'Science and Literature,' from *The Hope of Progress*, (London: Wildwood House, 1974).

6. Chris Fitter, *Radical Shakespeare: Politics and Stagecraft in the Early Career* (London: Routledge, 2012), p. 35.

7. Cited in Alan Sokal, 'Transgressing the Boundaries: An Afterword,' *Philosophy and Literature*, 20(2), 1996: 338-46.

8. Po-mo generator: http://www.elsewhere.org/pomo.

9. Mikhail Emelianov, 'How To Fake Your Way Through Hegel,' *Perverse Egalitarianism*, 9 June 2012: http://perve-galit.wordpress.com/2012/06/09/how-to-fake-your-way-through-hegel.

10. Woody Allen, 'My Philosophy,' *The Complete Prose of Woody Allen* (London: Picador, 1997), pp. 169-70.

11. Richard Ellmann, *James Joyce* (Oxford University Press, 1965), p. 60.

12. Ibid., p. 486.

13. Ibid., p. 715.

14. John Cowper Powys, *A Glastonbury Romance* (London: Macdonald, 1953/1933), p. 666.

15. John Goode, '1848 and the Strange Disease of Modern Love,' *Literature and Politics in the Nineteenth Century*, ed. John Lucas (London: Methuen, 1971), p. 61 (pp. 45-76); J. M. Bertram, *The New Zealand Letters of Thomas Arnold the Younger* (Oxford University Press), pp. 215-6.

16. Richard Ellmann, *James Joyce* (Oxford University Press, 1965), p. 563.

17. Ibid., p. 2.

18. James Joyce, *Ulysses*, ed. Jeri Johnson (Oxford University Press, 1998), pp. 310, 315.

19. Ibid., pp. 316, 319.

20. Ibid.

21. Ellmann, *James Joyce*, pp. 476-7; Joyce, *Ulysses*, p. 317.

22. Joyce, *Ulysses*, p. 319.

23. Stanislaus Joyce, *My Brother's Keeper*, ed. Richard Ellmann (London: Faber & Faber, 1958), p. 53.

24. Ellmann, *James Joyce*, p. 407.

25. Joyce, *Ulysses*, p. 34.

26. Ibid., pp. 24, 25.

27. Ibid., p. 155.

28. Ibid., pp. 156-7.

29. Ibid., pp. 179, 184

30. Joyce, *My Brother's Keeper*, pp. 53-4; *Ulysses*, p. 31; A. Norman Jeffares and Brendan Kennelly (eds.), *Joycechoyce: The Poems in Verse and Prose of James Joyce* (London: Kyle Cathie Limited, 1992), p. 38.

31. Fritz Senn, 'Book of Many Turns,' in Thomas Staley (ed.), *'Ulysses': Fifty Years* (Indiana University Press, 1974), p. 44.

32. Derek Attridge, 'Reading Joyce,' *The Cambridge Companion to James Joyce* [*CC*], ed. Derek Attridge (Cambridge University Press, 1990), p. 1; Joyce, *Ulysses*, pp. 323, 137.

33. Hugh Kenner, *Ulysses* (London: George Allen & Unwin, 1980), p. 62; Ellmann, *James Joyce*, p. 493.

34. Joyce, *Ulysses*, p. 633.

35. Norman Finkelstein, interview, New York, 14 March 2010, in Chris Hedges, 'Noam Chomsky Has Never Seen Anything Like This,' 19 April 2010, *The World As It Is: Dispatches on the Myth of Human Progress* (New York: Nation Books, 2013), pp. 97-8 (pp. 94-9).

36. Ellmann, *James Joyce*, p. 2.

37. Ibid., p. 661.

38. Thomas H. Bell, 'Oscar Wilde's Unwritten Play,' *Bookman*

(New York), April-May 1930.

39. Emer Nolan, *James Joyce and Nationalism* (London: Routledge, 1995), p. 134.

40. Joyce, *Ulysses*, p. 462.

41. Stephen Albert Rohs, *Eccentric Nation* (Madison: Fairleigh Dickinson University Press, 2009), p. 29.

42. Mary Colum, *Life and the Dream* (New York: Doubleday, 1947), p. 383.

43. James Joyce, *A Portrait of the Artist as a Young Man* (London: Granada, 1977), p. 222; 'Trust Not Appearances,' cited in Ellmann, p. 36.

44. Ellmann, *James Joyce*, pp. 476-7; Ernest Renan, *The Life of Jesus* (London: Trübner & Co., 1864), p. 112.

45. Joyce, *Ulysses*, p. 317.

46. 'Ireland: Island of Saints and Sinners,' in James Joyce, *Occasional, Critical, and Political Writing*, ed. Kevin Barry (Oxford University Press, 2000), p. 118 (108-26).

47. Slavoj Žižek, *The Ticklish Subject: The Absent Centre of Political Ontology* (London: Verso, 2000), p. 274.

48. Cited in Wayne Ellwood, *The No-Nonsense Guide to Globalization* (Oxford: New Internationalist Publications, 2009), p. 14.

49. Bertrand Russell, 'Property,' *The Basic Writings of Bertrand Russell, 1903-1959*, eds. Robert E. Egner and Lester E. Dennon (London: Routledge, 1999), p. 484.

50. Aldous Huxley, *Crome Yellow* (1921), ch. Xxii

51. Emmanuel Levinas, *Discovering Existence with Husserl*, trans. Richard A. Cohen and Michael B. Smith (Northwestern University Press, 1998), p. 19.

52. Rudolf Rocker, *Nationalism and Culture*, trans. Ray E. Chase (Los Angeles: Rocker Publications Committee, 1952), ch. 1.

53. Michael Albert, 'Science, post modernism and the left', *Z Magazine* 9(7/8), July/August 1996: 69 (64-9).

54. David Harvey, *A Brief History of Neoliberalism* (Oxford

University Press, 2005), p. 175,

55. Julian Baggini, 'Let's play Žižuku!' *Talking Philosophy*, 3 March 2008: http://blog.talkingphilosophy.com/?p=219.

56. Uri Gordon, *Anarchy Alive!: Anti-authoritarian Politics from Practice to Theory* (London: Pluto Press, 2008), p. 14.

57. Chris Hedges, 'The Man in the Mirror,' 13 July 2009, *The World As It Is: Dispatches on the Myth of Human Progress* (New York: Nation Books, 2013), pp. 44-5 (pp. 40-5).

58. Germaine Greer, 'Caster Semenya sex row: What makes a woman?' 20 August 2009, *Guardian*: http://www.the guardian.com/sport/2009/aug/20/germaine-greer-caster-semenya.

59. Wolfram Hinzen, *Mind Design and Minimal Syntax* (Oxford University Press, 2006).

60. Peter Kropotkin, *Memoirs of a Revolutionist* (1899), in Marshall S. Shatz (ed.), *The Essential Works of Anarchism* (New York: Quadrangle Books, 1972), p. 311.

61. Mikhail Bakunin, *God and the State*, in *The Essential Works of Anarchism*, p. 151.

62. Galen Strawson, *Real Materialism and Other Essays* (Oxford University Press, 2008), pp. 1-2.

63. John Cowper Powys, *Porius*, eds. Judith Bond and Morine Krisdóttir (London: Overlook Duckworth, 2007), p. 697.

64. Aldous Huxley, *Island* (London: Flamingo, 1994).

7. Merlin, Glastonbury, and Shakespearean Anarchism

1. R. D. Mullen, 'The complete text of a hitherto abridged masterpiece,' *Science Fiction Studies* 21(2), July 1994: 251 (251-2).

2. Lawrence Millman, 'An Irresistible Long-winded Bore', *The Atlantic*, August 2000: http://www.theatlantic.com/past/docs/issues/2000/08/millman.htm.

3. John Cowper Powys, *Porius*, eds. Judith Bond and Morine Krisdóttir (London: Overlook Duckworth, 2007), p. 260.

4. Ibid., p. 521.
5. Michael Sandel, *Liberalism and the Limits of Justice* (Cambridge University Press, 1980).
6. Peter Kropotkin, *Mutual Aid: A Factor in Evolution* London: Allen Lane, 1972), p. 22.
7. Powys, *Porius*, p. 25; John Cowper Powys, *A Glastonbury Romance* (London: Macdonald, 1953/1933), p. 848.
8. Ibid., p. 194.
9. Ibid., p. 116.
10. Ibid., p. 44.
11. David Foster Wallace, *Infinite Jest* (London: Abacus, 1997), p. 158, pp. 157-69.
12. Powys, *Porius*, p. 744.
13. John Cowper Powys, *In Defence of Sensuality* (London: Victor Gollancz, 1930), p. 241.
14. Cited in Ann M. Reed, 'From the Front Row,' ed. Melvon L. Ankey, *Powys Journal*, VII, 1997, p. 51 (emphasis his).
15. Ibid., p. 626.
16. Powys, *A Glastonbury Romance*, p. 995.
17. Russell, 'What I Believe,' *The Basic Writings of Bertrand Russell*, p. 367.
18. Chris Hedges, 'We Are Breeding Ourselves to Extinction,' 9 March 2009, *The World As It Is: Dispatches on the Myth of Human Progress* (New York: Nation Books, 2013), p. 280 (pp. 279-82).
19. Marshall S. Shatz (ed.), *The Essential Works of Anarchism* (New York: Quadrangle Books, 1972), p. xv.
20. John Cowper Powys, *Autobiography* (London: John Lane The Bodley Head, 1934), p. 323.
21. Judith Suissa, *Anarchism and Education: A Philosophical Perspective* (Oakland: PM Press, 2010), p. 106.
22. Shatz, *The Essential Works of Anarchism*, p. xvii.
23. Leon Trotsky, *The Russian Revolution* (1930).
24. Shatz, *The Essential Works of Anarchism*, p. xviii-xix.

25. Powys, *Autobiography*, pp. 626-7.
26. Powys, *A Glastonbury Romance*, pp. 72-3.
27. Ibid., p. 96.
28. Peter Kropotkin, *Modern Science and Anarchism* (London: Freedom Press, 2nd ed. 1923), p. 45.
29. Shatz, *The Essential Works of Anarchism*, p. xix.
30. Herbert Read, *Existentialism, Marxism and Anarchism* (1949), in *The Essential Works of Anarchism*, p. 534 (emphasis his).
31. Ibid., p. 538 (emphasis his).
32. John Cowper Powys, *Autobiography* (London: John Lane The Bodley Head, 1934), pp. 6-7.
33. Cited in Lawrence Millman, 'An Irresistible Long-winded Bore', *The Atlantic*, August 2000: http://www.theatlantic.com/past/docs/issues/2000/08/millman.htm.
34. Powys, *Autobiography*, pp. 23-4.
35. Powys, *A Glastonbury Romance*, p. 996.
36. John Cowper Powys, *Atlantis* (London: Macdonald, 1954), pp. 383, 448.
37. Powys, *Porius*, p. 34 (emphasis his).
38. Powys, *Autobiography*, p. 105.
39. Powys, *Porius*, pp. 136.
40. Ibid., p. 49.
41. Cited in Fernand Braudel, *Civilization and Capitalism 15th-18th Century*, vol. II, *The Wheels of Commerce*, trans. Sian Reynolds (University of California Press, 1992/1979), pp. 165-6.
42. Powys, *Porius*, p. 715.
43. Nicholas Birns, 'Awe-Inspiring Hideousness: Powys's Great Twentieth-Century Novel of the Fifth Century', *Hyperion* 5(2), November 2010: 157.
44. Powys, *Porius*, p. 146 (emphasis his).
45. Powys, *A Glastonbury Romance*, p. 372.
46. Ibid., p. 965; Donald Davidson, 'On the Very Idea of a Conceptual Scheme,' *Proceedings and Addresses of the*

American Philosophical Association, 47 (1973-1974): 5-20.

47. Powys, *Porius*, p. 495.

48. Ibid., p. 610.

49. Powys, *A Glastonbury Romance*, p. 612.

50. Ibid., pp. 704-5.

51. William Shakespeare, *Titus Andronicus*, 2.4, *The Complete Works*, ed. Stanley Wells, Gary Taylor, John Jowett and William Montgomery, 2nd ed. (Oxford University Press, 2005), p. 167.

52. Powys, *A Glastonbury Romance*, p. 1105.

53. Ibid., p. 1106.

54. J. M. Coetzee, *Slow Man* (London: Vintage, 2006), p. 13.

55. Powys, *Porius*, p. 160.

56. Ibid., p. 270.

57. Bernard Dick, review of *Porius*, *World Literature Today*, 68(4), Autumn 1994: 813.

58. Powys, *Porius*, pp. 260-1. See also Kathleen Blanchard, 'Power robs the brain of empathy,' 10 August 2013, *Digital Journal*: http://www.digitaljournal.com/article/356229.

59. Ibid., p. 260.

60. F. Schlegel, *Philosophical Fragments*, trans. P. Firchow (University of Minnesota Press, 1991), p. 53; William Shakespeare, *Henry VI, Part 1*, 3.6.

61. Chris Fitter, *Radical Shakespeare: Politics and Stagecraft in the Early Career* (London: Routledge, 2012), p. 12.

62. Victor Kiernan, *Shakespeare Poet and Citizen* (London: Verso, 1993), p. 37.

63. See in particular Edward Bond's Preface to *Lear* (London: Methuen, 1983).

64. Stephen Fry, *The Fry Chronicles* (London: Penguin, 2010), pp. 85-6; Fitter, *Radical Shakespeare*, p. 20.

65. Richard Strier, 'Faithful Servants: Shakespeare's Praise of Disobedience,' in Heather Dubrow and Richard Strier, *The Historical Renaissance* (University of Chicago Press, 1988),

pp. 119-20.

66. John Palmer, *Political Characters of Shakespeare* (London: Macmillan, 1948), pp. 318-9.

67. Shakespeare, *Henry VI, Part 2*, 4.7.37-38.

68. Ibid., 5.2.6.

69. Fitter, *Radical Shakespeare*, p. 80.

70. Ibid., p. 30.

71. Ibid., p. 34.

72. Ibid., p. 3.

73. Cited in ibid., pp. 4-5.

74. Cited in ibid, p. 6.

75. Mark Goldie, 'The unacknowledged republic: officeholding in early modern England,' in Tim Harris (ed.), *The Politics of the Excluded, c.1500-1850* (New York: Palgrave, 2001), pp. 153-94.

76. Fitter, *Radical Shakespeare*, p. 11.

77. Thomas Starkey, *A Dialogue between Pole and Lupset*, ed. T. F. Mayer (London: Royal Historical Society, 1989), pp. 110-1.

78. Lucien van der Walt, 'Debating black Flame, Revolutionary Anarchism and Historical Marxism,' *International Socialism*, 130, Spring 2011, www.isj.org.uk/?id=729.

79. Wayne Price, *The Abolition of the State: Anarchist and Marxist Perspectives* (Bloomington, Indiana: AuthorHouse, 2007), p. 172 (emphasis his).

80. Cited in George Woodcock, *Anarchism and Anarchists* (Ontario: Quarry Press, 1992), p. 214.

81. Powys, *A Glastonbury Romance*, p. 691.

82. Ibid., pp. 815-6.

83. John Cowper Powys, *Wolf Solent* (London: Penguin, 2000), p. 15.

84. Goodway, *Anarchist Seeds beneath the Snow*, p. 336.

85. David Cromwell, *Why Are We The Good Guys?: Reclaiming You Mind From the Delusions of Propaganda* (Winchester: Zero Books, 2012), p. 113.

86. James Joyce, *Ulysses*, ed. Jeri Johnson (Oxford University Press, 1998), p. 114; David Edwards and David Cromwell, *Guardians of Power: The Myth of the Liberal Media* (London: Pluto, 2006), p. 68.

87. John McGrath, *A Good Night Out: Popular Theatre: Audience, Class and Form* (London: Nick Hern Books, 1981/1996), p. 89.

88. Tzeporah Berman, 'Politicians need to listen to the people, not the polluters,' Climate rescue blog, Greenpeace International, 23 November 2011: http://www.green peace.org/international/en/news/Blogs/climate/politicians-need-to-listen-to-the-people-not-/blog/37985/. Cited in ibid.

89. *Morning Star*, 1 June 2011.

90. Aldous Huxley, *Literature and Science* (London: Chatto & Windus, 1963), p. 92.

91. Bertrand Russell, *Proposed Roads to Freedom* (New York: Blue Ribbon Books, 1919), pp. xi-xii; 'Philosophy and Politics,' *Unpopular Essays* (London: Routledge, 1995), p. 19.

92. Powys, *A Glastonbury Romance*, p. 529.

93. John Lucas, 'Politics and the poet's role,' *Literature and Politics in the Nineteenth Century*, ed. John Lucas (London: Methuen, 1971), p. 7 (pp. 7-43).

94. Chomsky, 'A Special Supplement: The Responsibility of Intellectuals,' *The New York Review of Books*, 23 February 1967.

95. Fred Branfman, 'When Chomsky wept,' *Salon*, 17 June 2012: http://www.salon.com/2012/06/17/when_chomsky_wept.

96. Edwards and Cromwell, *NEWSPEAK in the 21st Century*, p. 128.

97. Jean-Jacques Rousseau, *The Social Contract*, trans. Maurice Cranston (Harmondsworth: Penguin, 1979), p. 141.

98. Karl Marx, 'A Contribution to the Critique of Hegel's *Philosophy of Right*. Introduction,' in *Early Writings*, introduced by L. Colleti (Harmondsworth: Penguin, 1975), p. 247 (emphasis his).

99. Douglas Jay, Geoffrey Bing, H.J. Laski, Ian Mikardo, Harold Wilson and Richard Crossman, *The Road to Recovery: Fabian Society lectures given in the autumn of 1947* (London: Wingate, 1948), pp. 49-50.

100. Cited in Konstantin Mochulsky, *Dostoevsky: His Life and Work* (Princeton University Press, 1967), p. 641.

101. David Harvey, 'The Right to the City,' *New Left Review*, vol. 53, September-October 2008, p. 23.

102. 'Il faut decider: il est temps,' *Le Révolté*, 27 December 1879, cited in Caroline Cahm, *Kropotkin and the Rise of Revolutionary Anarchism 1872-1886* (Cambridge University Press, 1989), p. 131.

103. Cited in Roderick Frazier Nash, *The Rights of Nature: A History of Environmental Ethics* (University of Wisconsin Press, 1989), p. 8.

104. Cited in Noam Chomsky, 'Government in the future', talk given at the Poetry Center, New York City, 16 February 1970: http://anarchism.s3.amazonaws.com/Chomsky%20on%20Governemnt%20in%20the%20Future.pdf.

105. Powys, *A Glastonbury Romance*, p. 461.

106. Ibid., pp. 999-1000.

107. Simone Weil, 'Reflections on War,' *Left Review* (London, 1938), cited in Colin Ward, *Anarchy in Action* (London: Freedom Press, 2008/1973), p. 31.

108. Cited in Iain McGilchrist, *The Master and His Emissary: The Divided Brain and the Making of the Western World* (Yale University Press, 2010), p. 35

Index

Contemporary culture has eliminated both the concept of the public and the figure of the intellectual. Former public spaces – both physical and cultural – are now either derelict or colonized by advertising. A cretinous anti-intellectualism presides, cheerled by expensively educated hacks in the pay of multinational corporations who reassure their bored readers that there is no need to rouse themselves from their interpassive stupor. The informal censorship internalized and propagated by the cultural workers of late capitalism generates a banal conformity that the propaganda chiefs of Stalinism could only ever have dreamt of imposing. Zer0 Books knows that another kind of discourse – intellectual without being academic, popular without being populist – is not only possible: it is already flourishing, in the regions beyond the striplit malls of so-called mass media and the neurotically bureaucratic halls of the academy. Zer0 is committed to the idea of publishing as a making public of the intellectual. It is convinced that in the unthinking, blandly consensual culture in which we live, critical and engaged theoretical reflection is more important than ever before.